The Oatmeal COOKBOOK

Breads * *Entrées* * *Desserts and More*

Publications International, Ltd.

Pictured on the front cover: Double Cherry Crumbles *(page 90)*.
Pictured on the back cover *(left to right):* Chicken and Veggie Meatballs with Fennel *(page 132)*, Cobbled Fruit Bars *(page 102)* and Wild Rice Three Grain Bread *(page 16)*.

ISBN-13: 978-4127-9788-7
ISBN-10: 1-4127-9788-8

Library of Congress Control Number: 2009920598

Manufactured in China.

8 7 6 5 4 3 2 1

Microwave Cooking: Microwave ovens vary in wattage. Use the cooking times as guidelines and check for doneness before adding more time.

Preparation/Cooking Times: Preparation times are based on the approximate amount of time required to assemble the recipe before cooking, baking, chilling or serving. These times include preparation steps such as measuring, chopping and mixing. The fact that some preparations and cooking can be done simultaneously is taken into account. Preparation of optional ingredients and serving suggestions is not included.

Table of Contents

✳ Bountiful Bread Basket 4

✳ Creative Cookie Classics 24

✳ Breakfast-Time Favorites 48

✳ Fabulous Fruit Desserts 70

✳ Bar Cookie Bonanza 92

✳ Super Snackable Cakes 116

✳ Main Dish Magic 130

Acknowledgments 140

Index 141

✳ ✳ ✳

Makes 1 loaf

Three-Grain Bread

1 cup whole wheat flour
3/4 cup all-purpose flour
1 package rapid-rise active dry yeast
1 cup milk
2 tablespoons honey
1 tablespoon olive oil
1 teaspoon salt
1/2 cup uncooked old-fashioned oats
1/4 cup whole grain cornmeal, plus additional for dusting
1 egg beaten with 1 tablespoon water (optional)
1 tablespoon old-fashioned oats for topping (optional)

1. Combine whole wheat flour, all-purpose flour and yeast in large bowl. Stir milk, honey, olive oil and salt in small saucepan over low heat until warm (110° to 120°F). Stir milk mixture into flour mixture; beat with dough hook of electric mixer at high speed 3 minutes. Mix in oats and cornmeal at low speed. If dough is too wet, add additional flour by teaspoonfuls until it begins to come together.
2. Beat on medium speed 5 minutes after ball of dough forms. Place dough in large oiled bowl; turn once to coat. Cover; let dough rise in warm place about 1 hour or until puffy and does not spring back when touched.
3. Punch dough down and shape into 8-inch long loaf. Place on baking sheet lightly dusted with cornmeal. Cover; let rise in warm place about 45 minutes or until almost doubled.
4. Meanwhile, preheat oven to 375°F. Make shallow slash down center of loaf with sharp knife. Brush lightly with egg mixture and sprinkle with oats, if desired. Bake 30 minutes or until loaf sounds hollow when tapped (internal temperature 200°F). Remove to wire rack; cool completely.

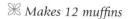

❋ Makes 12 muffins

Hearty Banana Carrot Muffins

2 ripe, medium DOLE® Bananas
1 package (14 ounces) oat bran muffin mix
³/₄ teaspoon ground ginger
1 medium DOLE® Carrot, shredded (¹/₂ cup)
¹/₃ cup light molasses
¹/₃ cup DOLE® Seedless or Golden Raisins
¹/₄ cup chopped almonds

❋ Mash bananas with fork (1 cup).

❋ Combine muffin mix and ginger in large bowl. Add carrot, molasses, raisins and bananas. Stir just until moistened.

❋ Spoon batter into paper-lined muffin cups. Sprinkle tops with almonds.

❋ Bake at 425°F 12 to 14 minutes until browned.

Prep Time: 20 minutes ❋ **Bake Time:** 14 minutes

> Oats of Wisdom: Light and dark molasses are interchangeable in recipes. Dark molasses has a slightly more robust flavor.

❋ *Makes 1 loaf*

No-Knead Sandwich Bread

¾ cup warm water (110° to 115°F)
2 packages (4½ teaspoons) active dry yeast
3 tablespoons canola oil
1 cup all-purpose flour
⅔ cup uncooked old-fashioned oats
¼ cup soy flour*
¼ cup wheat gluten*
¼ cup sesame seeds*
2 teaspoons sugar
1 teaspoon salt

Soy flour, wheat gluten and sesame seeds are available in the natural foods sections of many supermarkets and at health food stores.

1. Stir water and yeast in small bowl; let stand 5 minutes. Stir in oil.

2. Combine all-purpose flour, oats, soy flour, gluten, sesame seeds, sugar and salt in food processor fitted with plastic dough blade. Process until well blended using on/off pulsing action.

3. With processor running, slowly pour yeast mixture through feed tube; process until dough forms ball using on/off pulsing action. Unlock processor lid, but do not remove; let dough rise 1 hour or until doubled.

4. Spray 8×4-inch loaf pan with nonstick cooking spray. Process briefly until dough forms ball using on/off pulsing action. Turn dough out onto lightly floured work surface. Shape into disc. (Dough will be slightly sticky.) Roll dough on floured surface into 12×8-inch rectangle. Roll up from short side; fold ends under and place in prepared pan. Cover with towel; let rise in warm place 45 minutes or until doubled.

5. Preheat oven to 375°F. Bake 35 minutes or until bread is golden brown and sounds hollow when tapped. Remove to wire rack; cool completely. Cut into slices before serving.

No-Knead Sandwich Bread

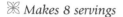

Oat and Whole Wheat Scones

1 cup uncooked old-fashioned oats
1 cup whole wheat flour
$^1/_2$ cup all-purpose flour
$^1/_4$ cup sugar
1 tablespoon baking powder
$^1/_4$ teaspoon salt
$^1/_2$ cup (1 stick) unsalted butter, cut into small pieces
$^1/_2$ cup whipping cream
1 egg
$^3/_4$ cup dried cherries

1. Preheat oven to 425°F. Line baking sheet with parchment paper; set aside.
2. Combine oats, flours, sugar, baking powder and salt in large bowl. Cut in butter with pastry blender or fork until mixture resembles coarse crumbs.
3. Beat cream and egg in small bowl; stir into flour mixture until dough comes together. Stir in cherries.
4. Turn dough out onto lightly floured surface. Shape dough into 8-inch round, about $^3/_4$ inch thick. Cut into 8 wedges. Place 1 inch apart on prepared baking sheet. Bake 18 minutes or until golden brown.

❋ *Makes 12 muffins*

Strawberry Muffins

1¹/₄ cups all-purpose flour
2¹/₂ teaspoons baking powder
 ¹/₂ teaspoon salt
  1 cup uncooked old-fashioned oats
 ¹/₂ cup sugar
  1 cup milk
 ¹/₂ cup (1 stick) butter, melted
  1 egg, beaten
  1 teaspoon vanilla
  1 cup chopped fresh strawberries

1. Preheat oven to 425°F. Grease bottoms only of 12 standard (2¹/₂-inch)
muffin cups or line with paper baking cups.
2. Combine flour, baking powder and salt in large bowl. Stir in oats and
sugar. Combine milk, butter, egg and vanilla in small bowl until well blended;
stir into flour mixture just until moistened. Fold in strawberries. Spoon into
prepared muffin cups.
3. Bake 15 to 18 minutes or until lightly browned and toothpick inserted into
centers comes out clean. Remove to wire rack; cool 10 minutes. Serve warm or
cool completely.

Savory Summertime Oat Bread

1½-POUND LOAF

Nonstick cooking spray
¼ cup finely chopped onion
1 cup water
2 tablespoons butter, softened
1 teaspoon salt
1½ cups all-purpose flour
¾ cup uncooked old-fashioned oats
¾ cup whole wheat flour
½ cup finely shredded carrots
1 tablespoon dried parsley flakes
1½ teaspoons active dry yeast

2-POUND LOAF

Nonstick cooking spray
⅓ cup finely chopped onion
1¼ cups water
3 tablespoons butter, softened
1½ teaspoons salt
2 cups all-purpose flour
1 cup uncooked old-fashioned oats
1 cup whole wheat flour
¾ cup finely shredded carrots
2 tablespoons dried parsley flakes
2 teaspoons active dry yeast

BREAD MACHINE DIRECTIONS

1. Spray small nonstick skillet with nonstick cooking spray. Cook onion over medium heat until transparent and soft, about 5 minutes. Set aside to cool.

2. Measuring carefully, place all ingredients, including cooled onion, in bread machine pan in order specified by owner's manual.

3. Program basic cycle setting and desired crust setting; press start. Immediately remove baked bread from pan; cool on wire rack.

❀ *Makes 12 servings*

Banana-Nana Pecan Bread

   1 cup QUAKER® Oats (quick or old fashioned, uncooked)
   ½ cup chopped pecans
   3 tablespoons margarine or butter, melted
   2 tablespoons firmly packed brown sugar
   1 (14-ounce) package banana bread quick bread mix
   1 cup water
   ½ cup mashed ripe banana
   2 eggs, lightly beaten
   3 tablespoons vegetable oil

Heat oven to 375°F. Grease and flour bottom only of 9×5-inch loaf pan. Combine oats, pecans, margarine and sugar; mix well. Reserve ½ cup oat mixture for topping; set aside. In bowl, combine remaining oat mixture, quick bread mix, water, banana, eggs and oil. Mix just until dry ingredients are moistened. Pour into prepared pan. Sprinkle top of loaf with reserved oat mixture. Bake 50 to 55 minutes or until wooden pick inserted into center comes out clean. Cool 10 minutes in pan; remove to wire rack. Cool.

> Oats of Wisdom: Don't throw away overripe bananas. Freeze bananas, in their peels, up to 6 months in a resealable food storage bag. Defrost to use in baked goods and smoothies.

※ *Makes 1 braided wreath or 2 loaves*

Wild Rice Three Grain Bread

1 package active dry yeast
$1/3$ cup warm water (105° to 115°F)
2 cups milk, scalded and cooled to 105° to 115°F
$1/2$ cup honey
2 tablespoons butter, melted
2 teaspoons salt
4 to $4^1/2$ cups bread flour or unbleached all-purpose flour
2 cups whole wheat flour
$1/2$ cup rye flour
$1/2$ cup uncooked rolled oats
1 cup cooked wild rice
1 egg, beaten with 1 tablespoon water
$1/2$ cup hulled sunflower seeds

In large bowl, dissolve yeast in water. Add milk, honey, butter and salt. Stir in 2 cups bread flour, whole wheat flour, rye flour and oats to make a soft dough. Add wild rice; cover and let rest 15 minutes. Stir in enough additional bread flour to make a stiff dough. Turn dough out onto board and knead 10 minutes. Add more flour as necessary to keep dough from sticking. Turn dough into lightly greased bowl; turn dough over to coat. Cover and let rise until doubled, about 2 hours. Punch down dough. Knead briefly on lightly oiled board. To shape dough, divide into 3 portions; roll into long strands. Braid strands and place on greased baking sheet in wreath shape, or divide in half and place each half in greased $9^1/2 \times 5^1/2$-inch loaf pans. Let rise until doubled, about 45 minutes. Brush tops of loaves with egg mixture; slash loaves if desired. Sprinkle with sunflower seeds. Bake at 375°F 45 minutes or until loaves sound hollow when tapped.

Favorite recipe from **Minnesota Cultivated Wild Rice Council**

Carrot and Oat Muffins

¹/₂ cup milk
¹/₂ cup unsweetened applesauce
 2 eggs, beaten
 1 tablespoon canola oil
¹/₂ cup shredded carrot
 1 cup minus 2 tablespoons uncooked old-fashioned oats
³/₄ cup whole wheat flour
³/₄ cup all-purpose flour
¹/₃ cup sugar
1¹/₂ teaspoons baking powder
 1 teaspoon ground cinnamon
¹/₂ teaspoon baking soda
¹/₄ teaspoon salt
¹/₄ cup finely chopped walnuts

1. Preheat oven to 350°F. Spray 12 standard (2¹/₂-inch) muffin cups with nonstick cooking spray.

2. Beat together milk, applesauce, eggs and oil in large bowl. Stir in carrot. Combine oats, whole wheat flour, all-purpose flour, sugar, baking powder, cinnamon, baking soda and salt in separate bowl. Stir well. Add flour mixture to applesauce mixture. Stir just until batter is moistened.

3. Spoon batter into prepared muffin cups. Sprinkle with walnuts. Bake 20 minutes or until muffins are golden brown. Cool 5 minutes in pan. Remove to wire rack; cool completely.

Note: These muffins are best eaten the same day.

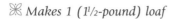

Good Morning Bread

¹/₄ cup water
1 cup mashed ripe bananas (about 3 medium)
3 tablespoons vegetable oil
1 teaspoon salt
2¹/₄ cups bread flour
³/₄ cup whole wheat flour
³/₄ cup chopped pitted dates
¹/₂ cup uncooked old-fashioned oats
¹/₄ cup nonfat dry milk powder
1 teaspoon grated orange peel (optional)
1 teaspoon ground cinnamon
2 teaspoons active dry yeast

BREAD MACHINE DIRECTIONS

1. Measuring carefully, place all ingredients in bread machine pan in order specified by owner's manual.

2. Program basic cycle and desired crust setting; press start. Immediately remove baked bread from pan; cool on wire rack.

Note: This recipe produces a moist, slightly dense loaf that has a lower volume than other loaves. The banana flavor is more prominent when the bread is toasted.

❋ Makes 16 slices

Soda Bread

1¹/₂ cups whole wheat flour
1 cup all-purpose flour
¹/₂ cup rolled oats
¹/₄ cup sugar
1¹/₂ teaspoons baking powder
¹/₂ teaspoon baking soda
¹/₄ teaspoon ground cinnamon
¹/₃ cup raisins (optional)
¹/₄ cup walnuts (optional)
1¹/₄ cups low-fat buttermilk
1 tablespoon vegetable oil

Preheat oven to 375°F. Combine whole wheat flour, all-purpose flour, oats, sugar, baking powder, baking soda and cinnamon in large bowl. Stir in raisins and walnuts, if desired. Gradually stir in buttermilk and oil until dough forms. Knead in bowl for 30 seconds. Spray 8×4-inch loaf pan with nonstick cooking spray; place dough in pan. Bake 40 to 50 minutes or until wooden toothpick inserted into center comes out clean.

*Favorite recipe from **The Sugar Association, Inc.***

Soda Bread

Creative Cookie Classics

Pumpkin Oatmeal Cookies

1 cup all-purpose flour
1 teaspoon ground cinnamon
$\frac{1}{2}$ teaspoon salt
$\frac{1}{2}$ teaspoon ground nutmeg
$\frac{1}{4}$ teaspoon baking soda
$1\frac{1}{2}$ cups packed light brown sugar
$\frac{1}{2}$ cup (1 stick) butter, softened
1 egg
1 teaspoon vanilla
$\frac{1}{2}$ cup solid-pack pumpkin
2 cups uncooked old-fashioned oats
1 cup dried cranberries (optional)

1. Preheat oven to 350°F. Line cookie sheets with parchment paper.

2. Sift flour, cinnamon, salt, nutmeg and baking soda into medium bowl. Beat brown sugar and butter in large bowl with electric mixer at medium speed about 5 minutes or until light and fluffy.

3. Beat in egg and vanilla. Add pumpkin; beat at low speed until blended. Beat in flour mixture just until blended. Add oats; mix well. Stir in cranberries, if desired. Drop dough by rounded tablespoonfuls 2 inches apart onto prepared cookie sheets.

4. Bake 12 minutes or until golden brown. Cool 1 minute on cookie sheets. Remove to wire racks; cool completely.

✳ ✳ ✳

Chocolate Oatmeal Chippers

1¼ cups all-purpose flour

½ cup NESTLÉ® TOLL HOUSE® Baking Cocoa

1 teaspoon baking soda

¼ teaspoon salt

1 cup (2 sticks) butter or margarine, softened

1 cup packed brown sugar

½ cup granulated sugar

1 teaspoon vanilla extract

2 eggs

1¾ cups (11½-ounce package) NESTLÉ® TOLL HOUSE® Milk
Chocolate Morsels

1¾ cups quick or old-fashioned oats

1 cup chopped nuts (optional)

PREHEAT oven to 375°F.

COMBINE flour, cocoa, baking soda and salt in medium bowl. Beat butter, brown sugar, granulated sugar and vanilla in large mixer bowl until creamy. Beat in eggs. Gradually beat in flour mixture. Stir in morsels, oats and nuts. Drop dough by rounded tablespoon onto ungreased baking sheets.

BAKE for 9 to 12 minutes or until edges are set but centers are still soft. Cool on baking sheets for 2 minutes; remove to wire racks to cool completely.

Bar Cookie Variation: PREHEAT oven to 350°F. Grease 15×10-inch jelly-roll pan. Prepare dough as above. Spread into prepared pan. Bake for 25 to 30 minutes. Cool in pan on wire rack. Makes about 4 dozen bars.

Gingery Oat and Molasses Cookies

1 cup all-purpose flour
3/4 cup whole wheat flour
1/2 cup uncooked old-fashioned oats
1 1/2 teaspoons baking powder
1 1/2 teaspoons ground ginger
1 teaspoon baking soda
1/2 teaspoon ground cinnamon
1/4 teaspoon salt
3/4 cup sugar
1/2 cup (1 stick) unsalted butter, softened
1/4 cup molasses
1 egg
1/4 teaspoon vanilla
1 cup chopped crystallized ginger
1/2 cup chopped walnuts

1. Grease cookie sheets; set aside. Combine flours, oats, baking powder, ground ginger, baking soda, cinnamon and salt in large bowl; set aside.
2. Beat sugar and butter in large bowl with electric mixer at high speed until light and fluffy. Beat in molasses, egg and vanilla. Gradually mix in flour mixture. Stir in crystallized ginger and walnuts. Shape into 2 logs about 10 inches long. Wrap in plastic wrap; chill 1 to 3 hours.
3. Preheat oven to 350°F. Cut 1/3-inch slices with sharp knife. Arrange 1 1/2 inches apart on prepared cookie sheets. Bake 12 to 14 minutes or until cookies are firm and browned at edges. Cool 5 minutes on cookie sheets. Remove to wire rack; cool completely.

Butterscotch Oatmeal Cookies

1¼ **cups all-purpose flour**
½ **teaspoon salt**
½ **teaspoon baking soda**
½ **cup butterscotch chips**
½ **cup (1 stick) butter, softened**
½ **cup packed brown sugar**
¼ **cup granulated sugar**
1 **egg, lightly beaten**
1 **teaspoon vanilla**
¾ **cup uncooked old-fashioned oats**
½ **cup shredded coconut**
½ **cup chopped pecans**
   Pecan halves (about 36)

1. Preheat oven to 350°F. Lightly grease cookie sheets.
2. Combine flour, salt and baking soda in medium bowl.
3. Place butterscotch chips in small microwavable bowl. Microwave on HIGH 1 minute; stir. Microwave at additional 30-second intervals until chips are melted and smooth.
4. Beat butter and sugars in large bowl with electric mixer at medium speed until light and fluffy. Add egg, melted butterscotch chips and vanilla; beat until well blended. Add flour mixture; beat just until blended. Stir in oats, coconut and chopped pecans.
5. Shape dough by level tablespoonfuls into balls; place 2 inches apart on prepared cookie sheets. Press 1 pecan half into center of each ball. Bake 10 to 12 minutes or until edges are lightly browned. Cool 1 minute on cookie sheets. Remove to wire racks; cool completely.

✳ *Makes about 4 dozen cookies*

Pineapple Oatmeal Cookies

   1 can (20 oz.) DOLE® Crushed Pineapple
1½ cups packed brown sugar
   1 cup butter or margarine, softened
   1 egg
   3 cups uncooked old-fashioned or quick cooking oats
   2 cups all-purpose flour
   1 teaspoon baking powder
   1 teaspoon ground cinnamon
 ½ teaspoon salt
   1 cup DOLE® Seedless or Golden Raisins
   1 cup chopped almonds, toasted (optional)

✳ Drain pineapple well; reserve ½ cup juice.

✳ Beat sugar and butter until light and fluffy in large bowl. Beat in egg, crushed pineapple and reserved juice.

✳ Combine oats, flour, baking powder, cinnamon, salt, raisins and almonds in medium bowl. Stir into pineapple mixture.

✳ Drop by heaping tablespoonfuls onto greased cookie sheets. Shape with back of spoon.

✳ Bake at 350°F 20 to 25 minutes or until golden. Cool on wire racks.

Prep Time: 20 minutes ✳ **Bake Time:** 25 minutes

Spiky Hedgehogs

1 package (about 18 ounces) refrigerated chocolate chip cookie dough
    with caramel filling in squares or rounds (20 count)
$^1\!/_2$ cup uncooked old-fashioned oats
$^1\!/_2$ cup all-purpose flour
$2^1\!/_2$ packages ($1^1\!/_2$ ounces each) chocolate-covered crisp wafer candy bars
$^2\!/_3$ cup creamy peanut butter
2 tablespoons butter or margarine
1 cup powdered sugar
$^1\!/_2$ teaspoon vanilla
2 to 3 tablespoons milk
1 cup flaked coconut, toasted*
Mini chocolate chips

To toast coconut, preheat oven to 350°F. Spread evenly on ungreased cookie sheet. Bake 5 to 7 minutes, stirring occasionally, until light golden brown.

1. Grease cookie sheets. Remove dough from wrapper; place in large bowl. Let dough stand at room temperature about 15 minutes.
2. Add oats and flour to dough in bowl; beat with electric mixer at medium speed until well blended.
3. Separate candy bars into individual sticks; cut sticks in half crosswise to make 20 pieces. Divide dough into 20 pieces. Wrap dough pieces around candy bar pieces, completely covering tops and sides. Place 2 inches apart on prepared cookie sheets; pinch one end of dough to make slightly pointed. Freeze 10 minutes or until firm.
4. Meanwhile, preheat oven to 350°F. Bake cookies 10 to 12 minutes or until firm and edges are lightly browned. Remove from oven. Cool 2 minutes on cookie sheets. Remove to wire rack; cool completely.
5. Beat peanut butter and butter in medium bowl with electric mixer at medium speed until well blended and smooth. Add powdered sugar and vanilla. Beat at medium speed, adding milk by tablespoons until mixture is of desired frosting consistency. Reserve 1 tablespoon frosting.
6. Frost tops and sides of cookies with remaining frosting, leaving pointed ends unfrosted. Place toasted coconut in shallow bowl. Dip frosted ends of cookies into toasted coconut to cover. Attach mini chocolate chips for eyes and nose on pointed end of each cookie with reserved frosting.

✳ *Makes about 4 dozen biscotti*

Oat, Chocolate and Hazelnut Biscotti

$1^{1}/_{2}$ **cups whole wheat flour**
  1 cup all-purpose flour
  1 cup uncooked old-fashioned oats
  2 teaspoons baking powder
  $^{1}/_{2}$ **teaspoon salt**
  $^{1}/_{2}$ **teaspoon ground cinnamon**
$1^{1}/_{2}$ **cups sugar**
  $^{1}/_{2}$ **cup (1 stick) unsalted butter, at room temperature**
  3 eggs
  1 teaspoon vanilla
  2 cups toasted whole hazelnuts
  $^{3}/_{4}$ **cup semisweet chocolate chunks**

1. Preheat oven to 325°F. Line cookie sheet with parchment paper.

2. Combine flours, oats, baking powder, salt and cinnamon in large bowl. Beat sugar and butter in large bowl with electric mixer at high speed until light and fluffy. Beat in eggs and vanilla. Gradually mix in flour mixture. Stir in hazelnuts and chocolate chunks.

3. Divide dough in half. Shape into logs 10 to 12 inches long; flatten slightly to 3-inch width. Place on cookie sheet. Bake 30 minutes. Cool completely on baking sheet.

4. *Reduce oven temperature to 300°F.* Transfer logs to cutting board. Cut diagonal slices about $^{1}/_{2}$ inch thick using serrated knife. Arrange slices on cookie sheet. Bake 10 to 15 minutes or until golden. Turn slices over and bake 5 to 10 minutes or until golden. Remove to wire rack; cool completely.

> Oats of Wisdom: To toast hazelnuts, preheat oven to 325°F. Spread hazelnuts on baking sheet. Toast 5 to 7 minutes; remove from oven. Place nuts in a kitchen towel and rub to remove skins.

✳ *Makes about 6 dozen cookies*

Oatmeal-Chip Crispies

2 cups all-purpose flour
1 teaspoon baking powder
1 teaspoon baking soda
½ teaspoon salt
1 cup packed brown sugar
1 cup (2 sticks) butter, softened
¾ cup granulated sugar
2 eggs
1 teaspoon grated orange peel
2 tablespoons orange juice
2 cups uncooked old-fashioned oats
1 cup dried cranberries
¾ cup white chocolate chips
¾ cup semisweet chocolate chips

1. Preheat oven to 350°F. Grease cookie sheets.

2. Combine flour, baking powder, baking soda and salt in medium bowl. Beat brown sugar, butter and granulated sugar in large bowl with electric mixer at medium speed 2 minutes. Add eggs, orange peel and orange juice; beat 1 minute. Add flour mixture; beat until well blended. Stir in oats, cranberries and chocolate chips until well blended.

3. Shape dough into 1-inch balls. Place 1½ inches apart on prepared cookie sheets. Flatten slightly to ⅜-inch thickness.

4. Bake 15 to 17 minutes or until lightly browned. Cool 2 minutes on cookie sheets. Remove to wire racks; cool completely.

Cookie Dough Bears

1 package (about 18 ounces) refrigerated sugar cookie dough
1 cup uncooked quick oats
Mini semisweet chocolate chips

1. Combine cookie dough and oats in medium bowl; mix well. Cover and freeze 15 minutes.

2. Meanwhile, preheat oven to 350°F. Lightly spray cookie sheets with nonstick cooking spray. For each bear, shape 1 (1-inch) ball for body and 1 (³/₄-inch) ball for head. Place body and head together on cookie sheet; flatten slightly. Form 7 small balls for arms, legs, ears and nose; arrange on bear body and head. Place 2 chocolate chips on each head for eyes. Place 1 chocolate chip on each body for belly button.

3. Bake 12 to 14 minutes or until edges are lightly browned. Cool bears 2 minutes on cookie sheets. Remove to wire racks; cool completely.

✳ *Makes about 3 dozen cookies*

Fudgy Oatmeal Butterscotch Cookies

1 package (18.25 ounces) devil's food cake mix
1¹/₂ cups quick-cooking or old-fashioned oats, uncooked
³/₄ cup (1¹/₂ sticks) butter, melted
2 large eggs
1 tablespoon vegetable oil
1 teaspoon vanilla extract
1¹/₄ cups "M&M's"® Chocolate Mini Baking Bits
1 cup butterscotch chips

Preheat oven to 350°F. In large bowl, combine cake mix, oats, butter, eggs, oil and vanilla until well blended. Stir in "M&M's"® Chocolate Mini Baking Bits and butterscotch chips. Drop by heaping tablespoonfuls about 2 inches apart onto ungreased cookie sheets. Bake 10 to 12 minutes. Cool 1 minute on cookie sheets. Cool completely on wire racks. Store in tightly covered container.

✳ Makes about 3¹/₂ dozen cookies

PB & J Thumbprint Cookies

2 cups uncooked old-fashioned oats
1¹/₃ cups plus 1 tablespoon all-purpose flour
³/₄ teaspoon baking soda
¹/₂ teaspoon baking powder
¹/₂ teaspoon salt
1 cup packed brown sugar
³/₄ cup (1¹/₂ sticks) butter, softened
¹/₄ cup granulated sugar
¹/₄ cup chunky peanut butter
1 egg
1 tablespoon honey
1 teaspoon vanilla
¹/₂ cup chopped peanuts, unsalted or honey-roasted
¹/₂ cup grape jelly or flavor of choice

1. Preheat oven to 350°F. Line cookie sheets with parchment paper.
2. Combine oats, flour, baking soda, baking powder and salt in medium bowl. Beat brown sugar, butter and granulated sugar in large bowl with electric mixer at medium speed until well blended. Beat at high speed until light and fluffy. Add peanut butter, egg, honey and vanilla; beat at medium speed until well blended. Gradually add flour mixture; beat just until blended. Stir in peanuts. Drop dough by rounded tablespoonfuls onto prepared cookie sheets.
3. Bake 10 minutes. Press center of each cookie with back of teaspoon to make a slight indentation; fill with about ¹/₂ teaspoon jelly. Bake 4 to 6 minutes or until puffed and golden. Cool 5 minutes on cookie sheets. Remove to wire racks; cool completely.

✳ ✳ ✳

Basic Oatmeal Cookies

2 cups uncooked old-fashioned oats
1¹/₃ cups all-purpose flour
³/₄ teaspoon baking soda
¹/₂ teaspoon baking powder
¹/₂ teaspoon salt
1 cup packed light brown sugar
³/₄ cup (1¹/₂ sticks) butter, softened
¹/₄ cup granulated sugar
1 egg
1 tablespoon honey
1 teaspoon vanilla

1. Preheat oven to 350°F. Line cookie sheets with parchment paper.

2. Combine oats, flour, baking soda, baking powder and salt in medium bowl. Beat brown sugar, butter and granulated sugar in large bowl with electric mixer at medium speed until light and fluffy. Add egg, honey and vanilla; beat until blended. Gradually add flour mixture, about ¹/₂ cup at a time; beat just until blended. Drop dough by tablespoonfuls about 2 inches apart on prepared cookie sheets.

3. Bake 11 to 15 minutes or until cookies are puffed and golden. *Do not overbake.* Cool 5 minutes on cookie sheets. Remove to wire racks; cool completely.

✳ Makes about 2½ dozen cookies

Double Chocolate Coconut Oatmeal Cookies

1 cup shortening

1¾ cups packed light brown sugar

3 eggs

2 teaspoons vanilla extract

1⅓ cups all-purpose flour

½ cup HERSHEY'S Cocoa

2 teaspoons baking soda

¼ teaspoon salt

½ cup water

3 cups uncooked old-fashioned oats or quick-cooking oats

2 cups (12-ounce package) HERSHEY'S SPECIAL DARK Chocolate Chips or HERSHEY'S Semi-Sweet Chocolate Chips, divided

2 cups MOUNDS® Sweetened Coconut Flakes, divided

1 cup coarsely chopped nuts

1. Beat shortening, brown sugar, eggs and vanilla in large bowl until well blended. Stir together flour, cocoa, baking soda and salt; add alternately with water to shortening mixture. Stir in oats, 1 cup chocolate chips, 1 cup coconut and nuts, blending well. Cover; refrigerate 2 hours.

2. Heat oven to 350°F. Lightly grease cookie sheet or line with parchment paper. Using ¼-cup ice cream scoop or measuring cup, drop dough about 4 inches apart onto prepared cookie sheet. Sprinkle cookie tops with remaining coconut. Top with remaining chocolate chips (about 9 chips per cookie); lightly press into dough.

3. Bake 10 to 12 minutes or until set (do not overbake). Cool slightly; remove from cookie sheet to wire rack. Cool completely.

✳ *Makes about 4 dozen cookies*

Double Striped Peanut Butter Oatmeal Cookies

¾ **cup REESE'S® Creamy Peanut Butter**
½ **cup (1 stick) butter or margarine, softened**
⅓ **cup granulated sugar**
⅓ **cup packed light brown sugar**
 1 **egg**
 2 **tablespoons milk**
 1 **teaspoon vanilla extract**
1⅓ **cups uncooked quick-cooking oats, divided**
 1 **cup all-purpose flour**
 1 **teaspoon baking soda**
½ **teaspoon salt**
½ **cup HERSHEY'S Milk Chocolate Chips**
 2 **teaspoons shortening (do not use butter, margarine, spread or oil)**
½ **cup REESE'S® Peanut Butter Chips**

1. Heat oven to 350°F. Beat peanut butter and butter in large bowl until well blended. Add granulated sugar and brown sugar; beat until fluffy. Add egg, milk and vanilla; beat well. Stir together ½ cup oats, flour, baking soda and salt; gradually beat into peanut butter mixture.
2. Shape dough into 1-inch balls. Roll in remaining oats; place on ungreased cookie sheet. Flatten cookies with tines of fork to form a crisscross pattern.
3. Bake 10 to 12 minutes or until lightly browned. Cool slightly; remove from cookie sheet to wire rack. Cool completely.
4. Place chocolate chips and 1 teaspoon shortening in medium microwave-safe container. Microwave at medium (50%) 30 seconds; stir. If necessary, microwave at medium an additional 10 seconds at a time, stirring after each heating, until chocolate is melted and smooth when stirred. Drizzle over cookies. Repeat procedure with peanut butter chips and remaining 1 teaspoon shortening. Allow drizzles to set.

✳ Makes about 4¹/₂ dozen cookies

Grandma's Old-Fashioned Oatmeal Cookies

2 cups sugar

1 cup shortening

2 eggs

3¹/₂ cups all-purpose flour

3 cups uncooked old-fashioned oats

1 teaspoon baking soda

1 teaspoon salt

1 teaspoon ground cinnamon

1 cup buttermilk

1 cup raisins

1. Preheat oven to 350°F. Lightly grease cookie sheets.

2. Beat sugar and shortening in large bowl with electric mixer at medium speed until creamy. Beat in eggs, one at a time, until mixture is light and fluffy.

3. Combine flour, oats, baking soda, salt and cinnamon in separate bowl. Beat into shortening mixture, ¹/₃ cup at a time, alternating with buttermilk until well blended. Stir in raisins.

4. Drop dough by rounded tablespoonfuls onto prepared cookie sheets. Bake 12 to 15 minutes or until lightly browned. Cool 2 minutes on cookie sheets. Remove to wire racks; cool completely. Store at room temperature in airtight containers.

✳ *Makes about 3¹/₂ dozen cookies*

Oatmeal S'Mores Cookies

²/₃ **cup mini marshmallows**
2 **cups uncooked old-fashioned oats**
1¹/₃ **cups all-purpose flour**
³/₄ **teaspoon baking soda**
¹/₂ **teaspoon baking powder**
¹/₂ **teaspoon salt**
1 **cup packed brown sugar**
³/₄ **cup (1¹/₂ sticks) butter, softened**
¹/₄ **cup granulated sugar**
1 **egg**
1 **tablespoon honey**
1 **teaspoon vanilla**
1 **cup semisweet chocolate chips**
³/₄ **cup coarse chocolate graham cracker crumbs**

1. Cut marshmallows in half. Spread on baking sheet; freeze 1 hour.
2. Preheat oven to 350°F. Line cookie sheets with parchment paper.
3. Combine oats, flour, baking soda, baking powder, and salt in medium bowl. Beat brown sugar, butter and granulated sugar in large bowl with electric mixer at medium speed until well blended. Beat at high speed until light and fluffy. Add egg, honey and vanilla; beat at medium speed until well blended. Gradually add flour mixture; beat just until blended. Stir in chocolate chips and marshmallows.
4. Drop dough by rounded tablespoonfuls onto prepared cookie sheets; sprinkle with graham cracker crumbs. Bake 14 to 16 minutes or until puffed and golden. Cool 5 minutes on cookie sheets. Remove to wire racks; cool completely.

Variation: To make sandwich cookies, spread 1 tablespoon marshmallow creme onto flat side of one cookie. Spread 1 tablespoon prepared chocolate fudge frosting on flat side of second cookie. Press cookies together lightly; repeat with remaining cookies, marshmallow creme and frosting. Makes about 20 sandwiches.

Breakfast-Time Favorites

※ *Makes 4 servings*

Tropical Fruit Breakfast Parfaits

4 containers (6 ounces each) vanilla yogurt
1 medium banana, mashed
2 tablespoons maple syrup
³/₄ to 1 teaspoon ground cinnamon
1 cup honey-sweetened oat flakes cereal
½ cup sweetened flaked coconut
1 can (8 ounces) crushed pineapple in juice, drained
2 cups strawberries, quartered
1 medium kiwi, peeled and diced

Stir yogurt, banana, syrup and cinnamon in medium bowl until well blended. Spoon about ⅓ cup into 4 parfait or wine glasses. Top each with equal parts oat flakes, coconut and fruit.

Variations: Substitute plain yogurt for vanilla yogurt. Substitute honey for maple syrup.

> Oats of Wisdom: Prepare yogurt mixture the night before. Cover and refrigerate until serving time.

Sunny Seed Bran Waffles

2 egg whites
1 tablespoon dark brown sugar
1 tablespoon canola or vegetable oil
1 cup milk
2/3 cup unprocessed wheat bran
2/3 cup uncooked quick oats
1 1/2 teaspoons baking powder
1/4 teaspoon salt
3 tablespoons toasted sunflower seeds*
1 cup apple butter

To toast sunflower seeds, cook and stir in small nonstick skillet over medium heat about 5 minutes or until golden brown. Remove from skillet.

1. Beat egg whites in medium bowl with electric mixer until soft peaks form; set aside. Mix sugar and oil in small bowl. Stir in milk; mix well. Combine bran, oats, baking powder and salt in large bowl; mix well. Stir sugar mixture into bran mixture. Add sunflower seeds; stir just until moistened. *Do not overmix.* Gently fold in beaten egg whites.
2. Spray nonstick waffle iron lightly with nonstick cooking spray; heat according to manufacturer's directions. Spoon 1/2 cup batter onto waffle iron for each waffle. Cook until steam stops escaping from around edges and waffle is golden brown. Serve each waffle with 1/4 cup apple butter.

Fruited Granola

3 cups uncooked quick oats
1 cup sliced almonds
1 cup honey
1/2 cup wheat germ or honey wheat germ
3 tablespoons butter or margarine, melted
1 teaspoon ground cinnamon
3 cups whole grain cereal flakes
1/2 cup dried blueberries
1/2 cup dried cranberries
1/2 cup dried banana chips

1. Preheat oven to 325°F.

2. Spread oats and almonds in single layer in 13×9-inch baking pan. Bake 10 to 15 minutes or until lightly toasted, stirring frequently.

3. Combine honey, wheat germ, butter and cinnamon in large bowl until well blended. Add oats and almonds; toss to coat completely. Spread mixture in single layer in baking pan. Bake 20 minutes or until golden brown. Cool completely in pan on wire rack. Break mixture into chunks.

4. Combine oat chunks, cereal, blueberries, cranberries and banana chips in large bowl. Store in airtight container at room temperature up to 2 weeks.

Oats of Wisdom: Prepare this granola on the weekend and you'll have a scrumptious snack or breakfast treat on hand for the rest of the week!

Banana Bread Oatmeal

    3 cups fat-free (skim) milk
    3 tablespoons packed brown sugar
    3/4 teaspoon ground cinnamon
    1/4 teaspoon ground nutmeg
    1/4 teaspoon salt (optional)
    2 cups QUAKER® Oats (quick or old fashioned, uncooked)
    2 medium-size ripe bananas, mashed (about 1 cup)
    2 to 3 tablespoons coarsely chopped toasted pecans
      Vanilla fat-free yogurt (optional)
      Banana slices (optional)
      Pecan halves (optional)

1. Bring milk, brown sugar, spices and salt, if desired, to a gentle boil in medium saucepan (watch carefully). Stir in oats. Return to a boil; reduce heat to medium. Cook 1 minute for quick oats, 5 minutes for old fashioned oats, or until most of liquid is absorbed, stirring occasionally.

2. Remove oatmeal from heat. Stir in mashed bananas and pecans. Spoon oatmeal into 4 cereal bowls. Top with yogurt, sliced bananas and pecan halves, if desired.

Cook's Tip: To toast nuts, spread in single layer on cookie sheet. Bake at 350°F about 6 to 8 minutes or until lightly browned and fragrant, stirring occasionally. Cool before using. Or spread in single layer on microwave-safe plate. Microwave on HIGH (100% power) 1 minute; stir. Continue to microwave on HIGH, checking every 30 seconds, until nuts are fragrant and brown. Cool before using.

✼ Makes 4 servings

Baked Oatmeal with Apricots

1 cup uncooked old-fashioned oats
1 teaspoon ground cinnamon, divided
1/4 teaspoon salt
1 1/2 cups milk
1 egg
2 tablespoons honey
2 teaspoons butter, melted
1 teaspoon vanilla
1 cup chopped peeled apple
3 tablespoons finely chopped dried apricots
1/4 cup chopped nuts (optional)

1. Preheat oven to 350°F. Lightly coat 1 1/2- to 2-quart baking dish with nonstick cooking spray.

2. Combine oats, 1/2 teaspoon cinnamon and salt in medium bowl. Combine milk, egg, honey, butter and vanilla in separate medium bowl; stir into oat mixture. Stir in apple and apricots.

3. Pour mixture into prepared baking dish. Sprinkle with remaining 1/2 teaspoon cinnamon. Bake 40 to 45 minutes or until knife inserted into center comes out clean. Let stand 5 minutes before serving. Sprinkle nuts over top, if desired.

Prep Time: 10 minutes ✼ **Cook Time:** 40 to 45 minutes

Honey Granola with Yogurt

$^1/_2$ cup uncooked old-fashioned oats
$^1/_4$ cup sliced almonds
2 tablespoons toasted wheat germ
1 tablespoon orange juice
1 tablespoon honey
$^1/_2$ teaspoon ground cinnamon
$1^1/_2$ cups whole strawberries
4 containers (6 ounces each) plain yogurt
1 teaspoon vanilla

1. Preheat oven to 325°F. Lightly spray 8-inch square baking pan with nonstick cooking spray.

2. Combine oats, almonds and wheat germ in small bowl. Combine orange juice, honey and cinnamon in another small bowl. Add juice mixture to oat mixture; mix well. Spread mixture evenly in prepared pan.

3. Bake 20 to 25 minutes or until toasted, stirring twice during baking. Spread mixture on large sheet of foil; cool completely.

4. Slice strawberries. Combine yogurt and vanilla in medium bowl. Layer yogurt mixture, granola and strawberries in clear dishes.

Prep Time: 10 minutes ⁂ **Bake Time:** 20 to 25 minutes

Oatmeal Pecan Pancakes

1¼ to 1½ cups milk, divided
½ cup uncooked old-fashioned oats
⅔ cup all-purpose flour
⅓ cup whole wheat flour
2½ tablespoons packed light brown sugar
2 teaspoons baking powder
½ teaspoon baking soda
¼ teaspoon salt
1 egg
2 tablespoons melted butter
½ cup chopped toasted pecans
Maple syrup (optional)

1. Bring ½ cup milk to a simmer in small saucepan. Stir in oats. Remove from heat; set aside 10 minutes.

2. Combine flours, brown sugar, baking powder, baking soda and salt in large bowl; mix well.

3. Combine egg and melted butter in small bowl; mix well. Stir in oatmeal mixture and ¾ cup milk. Add egg mixture to dry ingredients; stir just to combine. If mixture is too thick to spoon, add remaining ¼ cup milk, 1 tablespoon at a time. Add pecans; stir just to combine.

4. Lightly butter large skillet or griddle; heat over medium heat. Working in batches, drop batter by ¼ cupfuls. Cook about 2 minutes until tops are bubbly and bottoms are golden brown. Flip; cook until golden brown. Repeat with remaining pancake batter. Serve immediately.

Oatmeal Crème Brûlée

4 cups water
3 cups uncooked quick-cooking oats
$^1/_2$ teaspoon salt
6 egg yolks
$^1/_2$ cup granulated sugar
2 cups whipping cream
1 teaspoon vanilla
$^1/_4$ cup packed light brown sugar
    Fresh berries (optional)

SLOW COOKER DIRECTIONS

1. Coat slow cooker with nonstick cooking spray. Cover and set on HIGH to heat. Meanwhile, bring water to a boil. Immediately pour into preheated slow cooker. Stir in oats and salt. Cover.

2. Combine egg yolks and granulated sugar in small bowl. Mix well; set aside. Heat cream and vanilla in medium saucepan over medium heat until mixture begins to simmer. *Do not boil.* Remove from heat. Whisk $^1/_2$ cup hot cream into yolks, stirring rapidly so yolks don't cook.* Whisk warmed egg mixture into cream, stirring rapidly to blend well. Spoon mixture over oatmeal. Do not stir.

3. Turn slow cooker to LOW. Line lid with 2 paper towels. Cover; cook on LOW 3 to 3$^1/_2$ hours or until custard is set.

4. Uncover and sprinkle brown sugar over surface of custard. Line lid with 2 dry paper towels. Cover; continue cooking on LOW 10 to 15 minutes or until brown sugar has melted. Serve with fresh berries, if desired.

Place bowl on damp towel to prevent slipping.

Prep Time: 15 minutes **Cook Time:** 3 to 3$^1/_2$ hours

Oatmeal Crème Brûlée

Baked Cherry-Almond Oatmeal

2¼ cups QUAKER® Oats (quick or old fashioned, uncooked)
½ cup packed brown sugar
½ teaspoon salt
3 cups low-fat (2%) milk
3 eggs, lightly beaten
1 tablespoon melted butter (optional)
1 teaspoon vanilla
¼ to ½ teaspoon almond extract
¾ cup dried cherries
½ cup toasted sliced almonds
Vanilla low-fat yogurt

1. Heat oven to 350°F. Spray 8 (6-ounce) custard cups or ramekins with nonstick cooking spray; arrange on rimmed baking sheet.

2. Combine oats, brown sugar and salt in large bowl; mix well. Whisk together milk, eggs, butter, if desired, vanilla and almond extract in medium bowl. Add to dry ingredients; mix until well blended. Spoon into cups. Stir cherries into each cup, dividing evenly; sprinkle evenly with almonds.

3. Bake until knife inserted near center comes out clean, about 23 to 26 minutes for quick oats, 25 to 30 minutes for old fashioned oats. (Centers will not be completely set.) Cool 10 minutes. To serve, top with yogurt.

Variations: Substitute dried cranberries, blueberries or chopped dried apricots for dried cherries. To bake in 8-inch square baking pan, spray pan with nonstick cooking spray. Prepare oatmeal as directed. Pour into pan, stir in cherries and sprinkle with almonds. Bake until knife inserted near center comes out clean, about 30 to 35 minutes.

Cook's Tip: To toast nuts, spread in single layer on cookie sheet. Bake at 350°F about 6 to 8 minutes or until lightly browned and fragrant, stirring occasionally. Cool before using. Or spread in single layer on microwave-safe plate. Microwave on HIGH (100% power) 1 minute; stir. Continue to microwave on HIGH, checking every 30 seconds, until nuts are fragrant and brown. Cool before using.

✻ Makes 2 servings

Harvest Apple Oatmeal

1 cup water
1 cup unsweetened apple juice
1 medium apple, cored and chopped
1 cup uncooked old-fashioned oats
¼ cup raisins
⅛ teaspoon salt
⅛ teaspoon ground cinnamon
   Apple slices (optional)

MICROWAVE DIRECTIONS

1. Combine water, juice and chopped apple in 2-quart microwavable bowl. Microwave on HIGH 3 minutes, stirring halfway through cooking time.

2. Add oats, raisins, salt and cinnamon; stir until well blended.

3. Microwave on MEDIUM (50%) 4 to 5 minutes or until thick; stir before serving. Garnish with apple slices.

Conventional Directions: To prepare on the stove, bring water, apple juice and chopped apple to a boil in medium saucepan over medium-high heat. Stir in oats, raisins, salt and cinnamon until well blended. Cook, uncovered, over medium heat 5 to 6 minutes or until thick, stirring occasionally.

Caramel-Nut Sticky Biscuits

TOPPING

2/3 cup firmly packed brown sugar
1/4 cup light corn syrup
1/4 cup (1/2 stick) margarine, melted
1/2 teaspoon ground cinnamon
1 cup pecan halves

BISCUITS

2 cups all-purpose flour
1 cup QUAKER® Oats (quick or old fashioned, uncooked)
1/4 cup granulated sugar
1 tablespoon baking powder
3/4 teaspoon baking soda
1/2 teaspoon salt (optional)
1/2 teaspoon ground cinnamon
1/3 cup (51/3 tablespoons) margarine
1 cup buttermilk*

Sour milk can be substituted for buttermilk. For 1 cup sour milk, combine 1 tablespoon vinegar or lemon juice and enough milk to make 1 cup; let stand 5 minutes.

Heat oven to 425°F. For topping, combine first four ingredients; mix well. Spread onto bottom of 9-inch square baking pan. Sprinkle with pecans; set aside. For biscuits, combine dry ingredients; mix well. Cut in margarine with pastry blender or two knives until crumbly. Stir in buttermilk, mixing just until moistened. Knead gently on lightly floured surface 5 to 7 times; pat into 8-inch square. Cut with knife into sixteen 2-inch square biscuits; place over topping in pan. Bake 25 to 28 minutes or until golden brown. Let stand 3 minutes; invert onto large platter. Serve warm.

Chunky-Fruity Homemade Granola

2 cups uncooked old-fashioned oats
1⅓ cups raw, slivered almonds
1 cup sweetened, shredded coconut
¼ cup honey
3 tablespoons unsalted butter, melted
1 cup chopped dried apricots
¾ cup dried cranberries
¾ cup dried tart cherries
½ cup dried blueberries
½ cup roasted, unsalted cashew pieces
Plain yogurt (optional)

1. Preheat oven to 300°F. Line baking sheet with foil or parchment paper.
2. Combine oats, almonds and coconut in large bowl. Whisk honey and butter in small cup. Pour honey mixture over oat mixture and toss to coat evenly. Transfer mixture to prepared baking sheet, spreading evenly. Bake for 20 to 25 minutes or until golden, stirring once. Remove to wire rack; cool completely.
3. Combine remaining ingredients in large bowl. Add cooled oat mixture; stir to combine. Serve with yogurt, if desired.

> Oats of Wisdom: Store granola in airtight container for up to 2 weeks.

Oatmeal Brûlée with Raspberry Sauce

BRÛLÉE

4 cups water
1/2 teaspoon salt
3 cups uncooked old-fashioned oats
1 cup whipping cream
1/2 teaspoon vanilla
1/4 cup granulated sugar
3 egg yolks
3 tablespoons brown sugar

RASPBERRY SAUCE

6 ounces frozen sweetened raspberries
1/2 cup granulated sugar
1/4 cup water
1 teaspoon orange extract

1. Preheat oven to 300°F. Line baking sheet with foil.

2. Heat 4 cups water and salt in medium saucepan over high heat. Add oats; reduce heat to low. Cook and stir 3 to 5 minutes or until water is absorbed and oats are tender. Divide oatmeal among 4 large ramekins or ovenproof bowls. Place on prepared baking sheet.

3. Heat cream in another medium saucepan over high heat. *Do not boil.* Remove from heat; stir in vanilla. Whisk 1/4 cup granulated sugar and egg yolks in small bowl. Pour about 1/2 cup hot cream in thin stream into egg mixture, whisking quickly. Stir egg mixture into saucepan of hot cream, whisking until well blended and smooth. Ladle cream mixture equally over oatmeal in ramekins. Bake 35 minutes or until nearly set. Remove from oven; preheat broiler to 500°F.

4. Meanwhile, blend raspberries, 1/2 cup granulated sugar, 1/4 cup water and orange extract in blender until smooth. Pour sauce through strainer to remove seeds; discard seeds.

5. Sprinkle custards evenly with brown sugar. Broil 3 to 5 minutes or until tops are caramelized. Cool 5 to 10 minutes before serving. Serve with raspberry sauce.

Note: This brûlée has the texture of rice pudding and the taste of sweet custard, with a creme brûlée-like topping. *Brûlée* (broo-LAY) comes from the French word for "burned."

Fabulous Fruit Desserts

Strawberry and Peach Crisp

1 cup frozen unsweetened peach slices, thawed and cut into 1-inch pieces
1 cup sliced fresh strawberries
3 teaspoons sugar, divided
$1/4$ cup bran cereal flakes
2 tablespoons uncooked old-fashioned oats
1 tablespoon all-purpose flour
$1/8$ teaspoon ground cinnamon
$1/8$ teaspoon salt
1 tablespoon unsalted butter, cut into small pieces

1. Preheat oven to 325°F. Coat 1- to $1^1/2$-quart glass baking dish with nonstick cooking spray. Set aside.

2. Combine peaches, strawberries and 1 teaspoon sugar in medium bowl. Transfer to prepared baking dish.

3. Combine cereal, oats, flour, remaining 2 teaspoons sugar, cinnamon and salt in small bowl. Add butter; stir with fork until mixture resembles coarse crumbs. Sprinkle over fruit. Bake 20 minutes or until fruit is heated through and topping is slightly browned.

Variation: If you like the flavor of brown sugar, you may substitute 2 teaspoons of packed brown sugar for the 2 teaspoons of granulated sugar in the topping.

Variation: To make a strawberry crisp, omit the peaches and use 2 cups strawberries in the recipe.

❋ ❋ ❋

✳ *Makes 8 servings*

Apple Cinnamon Rice Crisp

    1 cup MINUTE® White or Brown Rice, uncooked
       Nonstick cooking spray
    1 can (20 ounces) apple pie filling
    1 cup packed brown sugar, divided
 $\frac{1}{2}$ cup raisins
 $\frac{1}{2}$ cup walnuts, chopped
    1 teaspoon ground cinnamon
 $1\frac{1}{2}$ cups uncooked rolled oats
    4 tablespoons margarine
       Vanilla ice cream (optional)

Prepare rice according to package directions. Preheat oven to 350°F. Spray 2-quart baking dish with nonstick cooking spray. Combine rice, pie filling, $\frac{1}{2}$ cup brown sugar, raisins, walnuts and cinnamon in medium bowl. Pour into prepared dish. In same bowl, combine remaining $\frac{1}{2}$ cup brown sugar and rolled oats. Cut in margarine with pastry blender or fork, mixing well until mixture is moist. Sprinkle over rice mixture. Bake 20 minutes. Serve with ice cream, if desired.

❋ *Makes 6 to 8 servings*

Apple Crumble Pot

FILLING

  ²/₃ **cup packed dark brown sugar**
  2 **tablespoons biscuit baking mix**
1½ **teaspoons ground cinnamon**
  ¼ **teaspoon ground allspice**
  4 **Granny Smith apples (about 2 pounds), cored and cut into**
      8 wedges each
  ½ **cup dried cranberries**
  2 **tablespoons butter, cubed**
  1 **teaspoon vanilla**

TOPPING

  1 **cup biscuit baking mix**
  ½ **cup uncooked old-fashioned oats**
  ⅓ **cup packed dark brown sugar**
  3 **tablespoons cold butter, cubed**
  ½ **cup chopped pecans**

SLOW COOKER DIRECTIONS

1. Coat slow cooker with nonstick cooking spray. Combine ²/₃ cup brown sugar, 2 tablespoons baking mix, cinnamon and allspice in large bowl. Add remaining filling ingredients; toss to coat. Transfer to slow cooker.

2. Combine 1 cup baking mix, oats and ½ cup brown sugar in large bowl. Cut in butter with pastry blender or 2 knives until mixture resembles pea-sized crumbs. Sprinkle evenly over filling; top with pecans. Cover; cook on HIGH 2¼ hours or until apples are tender. *Do not overcook.*

3. Turn off slow cooker. Uncover and let stand 15 to 30 minutes before serving. Garnish as desired.

Prep Time: 15 minutes ❋ **Cook Time:** 2¼ hours

✳ *Makes 6 servings*

Cranberry Peach Almond Dessert

2 bags (16 ounces each) frozen unsweetened peach slices
1 cup dried sweetened cranberries
1 teaspoon vanilla
$\frac{1}{2}$ teaspoon almond extract (optional)
$\frac{1}{2}$ cup uncooked old-fashioned oats
$\frac{1}{3}$ cup packed dark brown sugar
$\frac{1}{4}$ cup all-purpose flour
$\frac{1}{2}$ teaspoon ground cinnamon
$\frac{1}{4}$ cup ($\frac{1}{2}$ stick) cold butter
$\frac{1}{4}$ cup slivered almonds

1. Preheat oven to 350°F. Thaw peaches; do not drain. Transfer fruit to 9-inch deep dish pie pan or baking pan. Stir in cranberries, vanilla and almond extract, if desired.

2. Combine oats, brown sugar, flour and cinnamon in medium bowl. Cut in butter with pastry blender or 2 knives until mixture resembles coarse crumbs. Stir in almonds; sprinkle mixture evenly over peaches.

3. Bake 40 minutes or until peaches are tender and topping is golden brown.

Oats 'n' Apple Tart

1¹/₂ cups uncooked quick oats
¹/₂ cup packed brown sugar, divided
1 tablespoon plus ¹/₄ teaspoon ground cinnamon, divided
5 tablespoons butter or margarine, melted
2 medium Golden Delicious apples, cored and thinly sliced
1 teaspoon lemon juice
¹/₄ cup water
1 envelope unflavored gelatin
¹/₂ cup apple juice concentrate
1 package (8 ounces) cream cheese, softened
¹/₈ teaspoon ground nutmeg

1. Preheat oven to 350°F. Combine oats, ¹/₄ cup brown sugar and 1 tablespoon cinnamon in medium bowl. Add butter and stir until combined. Press onto bottom and up side of 9-inch pie plate. Bake 7 minutes or until set. Cool on wire rack.

2. Toss apple slices with lemon juice in small bowl; set aside. Place water in small saucepan. Sprinkle gelatin over water; let stand 3 to 5 minutes. Add apple juice concentrate; cook and stir over medium heat until gelatin is dissolved. *Do not boil.* Remove from heat; set aside.

3. Beat cream cheese in medium bowl with electric mixer at medium speed until fluffy and smooth. Add remaining ¹/₄ cup brown sugar, ¹/₄ teaspoon cinnamon and nutmeg. Mix until smooth. Slowly beat in gelatin mixture on low speed until blended and creamy, about 1 minute. *Do not overbeat.*

4. Arrange apple slices in crust. Spread cream cheese mixture evenly over top. Refrigerate 2 hours or until set.

❋ *Makes 2 servings*

Mixed Berry Crunch

1 tablespoon plus 2 teaspoons granulated sugar, divided
1 tablespoon cornstarch*
2 cups mixed berries (thawed if frozen)
½ cup uncooked old-fashioned oats
¼ cup packed brown sugar
2 tablespoons all-purpose flour
½ teaspoon cinnamon
⅛ teaspoon salt
⅛ teaspoon ground ginger
3 tablespoons cold butter

Increase to 2 tablespoons if using frozen berries.

1. Preheat oven to 375°F.

2. Combine 2 teaspoons granulated sugar and cornstarch in medium bowl. Add berries; toss to coat evenly. Divide berry mixture between 2 (5-inch) baking dishes.

3. For topping, combine oats, brown sugar, flour, remaining 1 tablespoon granulated sugar, cinnamon, salt and ginger in small bowl. Cut in butter using pastry blender or 2 knives until mixture resembles coarse crumbs. Sprinkle topping evenly over berries. Bake 20 to 25 minutes or until topping is golden brown. Serve warm with vanilla ice cream, if desired.

✳ Makes 6 servings

Apple-Date Upside-Down Tart

6 cups thinly sliced peeled Golden Delicious apples (about 6 medium)
2 teaspoons lemon juice
$^1/_3$ cup chopped dates
1$^1/_3$ cups uncooked quick oats
$^1/_2$ cup all-purpose flour
$^1/_2$ cup packed light brown sugar
$^1/_2$ teaspoon ground cinnamon
$^1/_4$ teaspoon ground ginger
$^1/_4$ teaspoon salt
    Dash ground nutmeg
    Dash ground cloves (optional)
$^1/_4$ cup ($^1/_2$ stick) cold butter, cut into small pieces

SLOW COOKER DIRECTIONS

1. Spray slow cooker with nonstick cooking spray. Place apples in medium bowl. Sprinkle with lemon juice; toss to coat. Add dates and mix well. Transfer apple mixture to slow cooker.

2. Combine oats, flour, brown sugar, cinnamon, ginger, salt, nutmeg and cloves, if desired, in medium bowl. Cut in butter with pastry blender or 2 knives until mixture resembles coarse crumbs.

3. Sprinkle oat mixture over apples; smooth top. Cover; cook on LOW 4 hours or HIGH 2 hours or until apples are tender.

Makes 10 to 12 servings

Cinnamon Pear Crisp

8 medium pears, peeled, cored and sliced
3/4 cup frozen unsweetened apple juice concentrate, thawed
1/2 cup golden raisins
1/4 cup plus 3 tablespoons all-purpose flour, divided
1 teaspoon ground cinnamon
1/3 cup uncooked quick oats
3 tablespoons packed dark brown sugar
3 tablespoons butter, melted

1. Preheat oven to 375°F. Spray 11×7-inch baking dish with nonstick cooking spray.
2. Combine pears, apple juice concentrate, raisins, 3 tablespoons flour and cinnamon in large bowl; mix well. Spoon mixture into prepared dish.
3. Combine oats, remaining 1/4 cup flour, brown sugar and butter in medium bowl; mix until coarse crumbs form. Sprinkle evenly over pear mixture. Bake 1 hour or until golden brown. Cool in pan on wire rack.

Makes 8 servings

Rhubarb Tart

Pastry for single-crust 9-inch pie
4 cups sliced (1/2-inch pieces) fresh rhubarb
1 1/4 cups sugar
1/4 cup all-purpose flour
2 tablespoons butter, cut into chunks
1/4 cup uncooked old-fashioned oats

1. Preheat oven to 450°F. Line 9-inch pie plate with pastry.
2. Combine rhubarb, sugar and flour in medium bowl; place in pie crust. Top with butter. Sprinkle with oats.
3. Bake 10 minutes. *Reduce oven temperature to 350°F.* Bake 40 minutes or until bubbly.

※ *Makes 4 servings*

Peach and Blueberry Crisp

3 cups fresh or thawed frozen sliced peeled peaches, undrained
1 cup fresh or thawed frozen blueberries, undrained
2 tablespoons granulated sugar
$1/4$ teaspoon ground nutmeg
2 tablespoons uncooked old-fashioned oats
2 tablespoons crisp rice cereal
2 tablespoons all-purpose flour
1 tablespoon packed brown sugar
1 tablespoon butter, melted
$1/8$ teaspoon ground cinnamon

1. Preheat oven to 375°F. Combine peaches and blueberries in ungreased 8-inch round baking dish. Combine granulated sugar and nutmeg in small bowl. Sprinkle over fruit; toss gently to combine.

2. Combine oats, rice cereal, flour, brown sugar, butter and cinnamon in small bowl. Sprinkle over fruit. Bake, uncovered, 35 to 40 minutes or until peaches are tender and topping is golden brown.

Variation: Try baking this crisp in 4 individual ramekins. Reduce baking time to 25 to 30 minutes.

Apple Toffee Crisp

5 cups (about 5 medium apples) peeled and sliced Granny Smith apples
5 cups (about 5 medium apples) peeled and sliced McIntosh apples
1¼ cups sugar, divided
1¼ cups all-purpose flour, divided
¾ cup (1½ sticks) butter or margarine, divided
1⅓ cups (8-ounce package) HEATH® BITS 'O BRICKLE® Toffee Bits
1 cup uncooked rolled oats
½ teaspoon ground cinnamon
¼ teaspoon baking powder
¼ teaspoon baking soda
¼ teaspoon salt
Whipped topping or ice cream (optional)

1. Heat oven to 375°F. Grease 13×9×2-inch baking pan.
2. Toss apple slices, ¾ cup sugar and ¼ cup flour in large bowl, coating apples evenly. Spread in bottom of prepared pan. Dot with ¼ cup (½ stick) butter.
3. Stir together toffee bits, oats, remaining ½ cup sugar, remaining 1 cup flour, cinnamon, baking powder, baking soda and salt. Melt remaining ½ cup (1 stick) butter; add to oat mixture, mixing until crumbs are formed. Sprinkle crumb mixture over apples.
4. Bake 45 to 50 minutes or until topping is lightly browned and apples are tender. Serve warm with whipped topping or ice cream, if desired. Cover; refrigerate leftovers.

❋ *Makes one 9-inch tart*

Rustic Plum Tart

¼ cup (½ stick) plus 1 tablespoon butter, divided
3 cups plum wedges (about 6 plums, see Tip)
¼ cup granulated sugar
½ cup all-purpose flour
½ cup uncooked old-fashioned oats
¼ cup packed brown sugar
½ teaspoon ground cinnamon
¼ teaspoon salt
1 egg
1 teaspoon water
1 refrigerated pie crust (half of 15-ounce package)
1 tablespoon chopped crystallized ginger

1. Preheat oven to 425°F. Line baking sheet with parchment paper.

2. Melt 1 tablespoon butter in large skillet over high heat. Add plums; cook and stir about 3 minutes or until plums begin to break down. Stir in granulated sugar; cook 1 minute or until juices have thickened. Remove from heat; set aside.

3. Combine flour, oats, brown sugar, cinnamon and salt in medium bowl. Cut in remaining ¼ cup butter with pastry blender or 2 knives until mixture resembles coarse crumbs.

4. Beat egg and water in small bowl. Unroll pie crust on prepared baking sheet. Brush crust lightly with egg mixture. Sprinkle with ¼ cup oat mixture, leaving 2-inch border around edge of crust. Spoon plums over oat mixture, leaving juices in skillet. Sprinkle with ginger. Fold crust up around plums, overlapping as necessary. Sprinkle with remaining oat mixture. Brush edge of crust with egg mixture.

5. Bake 25 minutes or until golden brown. Cool slightly before serving.

> Oats of Wisdom: For this recipe, use dark reddish-purple plums and cut the fruit into 8 wedges.

Double Cherry Crumbles

½ (about 18-ounce) package refrigerated oatmeal raisin cookie dough*
½ cup uncooked old-fashioned oats
¾ teaspoon ground cinnamon
½ teaspoon ground ginger
 2 tablespoons cold butter, cut into small pieces
 1 cup chopped pecans, toasted**
 1 bag (16 ounces) frozen pitted unsweetened dark sweet cherries, thawed
 2 cans (21 ounces each) cherry pie filling

*Save remaining ½ package of dough for another use.

**To toast pecans, spread in single layer on baking sheet. Bake in preheated 350°F oven 7 to 10 minutes or until golden brown, stirring frequently.

1. Let dough stand at room temperature about 15 minutes. Preheat oven to 350°F. Lightly grease 8 (½-cup) ramekins; place on baking sheet.

2. For topping, beat dough, oats, cinnamon and ginger in large bowl with electric mixer at medium speed until well blended. Cut in butter with pastry blender or 2 knives until large crumbs form. Stir in pecans.

3. Combine cherries and pie filling in large bowl. Divide cherry mixture evenly among prepared ramekins; sprinkle with topping. Bake about 25 minutes or until topping is browned. Serve warm.

Bar Cookie Bonanza

❋ *Makes about 2 dozen bars*

Oatmeal Date Bars

2 packages (about 18 ounces each) refrigerated oatmeal raisin
    cookie dough
2¹/₂ cups uncooked old-fashioned oats, divided
2 packages (8 ounces each) chopped dates
1 cup water
¹/₂ cup sugar
1 teaspoon vanilla

1. Let doughs stand at room temperature about 15 minutes. Preheat oven to
350°F. Lightly grease 13×9-inch baking pan.

2. Combine three fourths of one package of dough and 1 cup oats in medium
bowl; beat until well blended. Set aside.

3. Combine remaining 1¹/₄ packages dough and remaining 1¹/₂ cups oats
in large bowl; beat until well blended. Press dough evenly onto bottom of
prepared pan. Bake 10 minutes.

4. Meanwhile, combine dates, water and sugar in medium saucepan; bring
to a boil over high heat. Boil 3 minutes; remove from heat and stir in vanilla.
Spread date mixture evenly over partially baked crust; sprinkle evenly with
topping mixture.

5. Bake 25 to 28 minutes or until bubbly. Cool completely in pan on wire rack.

Cranberry Coconut Bars

FILLING

    2 cups fresh or frozen cranberries
    1 cup dried sweetened cranberries
    ²/₃ cup granulated sugar
    ¹/₄ cup water
    Grated peel of 1 lemon

CRUST

    1¹/₄ cups all-purpose flour
    ³/₄ cup uncooked old-fashioned oats
    ¹/₂ teaspoon baking soda
    ¹/₂ teaspoon salt
    1 cup packed light brown sugar
    ³/₄ cup (1¹/₂ sticks) unsalted butter, softened
    1 cup shredded sweetened coconut
    1 cup chopped pecans, toasted*

*To toast pecans, spread in single layer on baking sheet. Bake in preheated 350°F oven 5 to 7 minutes or until golden brown, stirring frequently.

1. Preheat oven to 400°F. Grease and flour 13×9-inch baking pan.

2. Combine fresh cranberries, dried cranberries, granulated sugar, water and lemon peel in medium saucepan. Cook and stir over medium-high heat 10 to 15 minutes until mixture is pulpy. Mash cranberries with back of spoon. Cool to lukewarm.

3. Combine flour, oats, baking soda and salt in medium bowl. Beat brown sugar and butter in large bowl with electric mixer at medium speed until creamy. Add flour mixture; beat just until blended. Stir in coconut and pecans. Reserve 1¹/₂ cups; pat remaining crumb mixture in bottom of prepared pan. Bake 10 minutes.

4. Gently spread cranberry filling evenly over crust. Sprinkle with reserved crumb mixture. Bake 18 to 20 minutes or until bars are set and crust is golden brown. Cool completely in pan on wire rack before cutting into bars.

Note: You can make these bars when fresh or frozen cranberries aren't available. Prepare the filling using 2 cups dried sweetened cranberries, 1 cup water and the peel of 1 lemon; cook and stir over medium heat 8 to 10 minutes. Use as directed in step 4.

✳ *Makes 3 dozen bars*

Pear Hazelnut Bars

1 recipe Basic Short Dough (page 106)
4 cups chopped, peeled, fresh pears
$^1/_2$ cup raisins
2 tablespoons fresh lemon juice
2 tablespoons all-purpose flour
2 tablespoons granulated sugar
1 teaspoon grated lemon peel
$^1/_2$ teaspoon ground cinnamon

CRUMB TOPPING
$^1/_2$ cup all-purpose flour
$^1/_2$ cup packed brown sugar
$^1/_2$ teaspoon ground cinnamon
$^1/_2$ cup (1 stick) cold butter, cubed
$^1/_2$ cup uncooked old-fashioned oats
$^1/_2$ cup chopped hazelnuts

1. Preheat oven to 350°F. Line 13×9-inch baking pan with foil, leaving 1-inch overhang. Spray foil with nonstick cooking spray.

2. Prepare Basic Short Dough. Press dough evenly into pan. Bake 25 minutes or until lightly browned. Set aside on wire rack.

3. Meanwhile, mix pears, raisins, lemon juice, 2 tablespoons flour, granulated sugar, lemon peel and $^1/_2$ teaspoon cinnamon in large bowl. Spread over warm crust.

4. Combine $^1/_2$ cup flour, brown sugar and remaining $^1/_2$ teaspoon cinnamon in medium bowl. Cut in butter with pastry blender or 2 knives until mixture resembles coarse crumbs. Stir in oats and hazelnuts. Sprinkle topping evenly over filling, lightly pressing into place.

5. Bake 30 minutes or until topping is golden brown. Cool completely in pan on wire rack.

6. Refrigerate bars at least 2 hours before serving. Remove foil from bars; cut into squares. Cut each square diagonally into triangles. Store covered in refrigerator.

Makes 2 to 3 dozen bars

Chocolate 'n' Oat Bars

1 cup all-purpose flour
1 cup uncooked quick-cooking oats
¾ cup firmly packed light brown sugar
½ cup (1 stick) butter or margarine, softened
1 (14-ounce) can EAGLE BRAND® Sweetened Condensed Milk (NOT evaporated milk)
1 cup chopped nuts
1 cup (6 ounces) semisweet chocolate chips

1. Preheat oven to 350°F (325°F for glass dish). In large bowl, combine flour, oats, brown sugar and butter; mix well. (Mixture will be crumbly.) Reserve ½ cup oat mixture and press remainder on bottom of 13×9-inch baking pan. Bake 10 minutes.
2. Pour EAGLE BRAND® evenly over crust. Sprinkle with nuts and chocolate chips. Top with reserved oat mixture; press down firmly.
3. Bake 25 minutes or until lightly browned. Cool. Chill if desired. Cut into bars. Store leftovers covered at room temperature.

Prep Time: 15 minutes **Bake Time:** 35 minutes

Chocolate 'n' Oat Bars

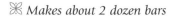

Ooey-Gooey Caramel Peanut Butter Bars

1 package (about 18 ounces) yellow cake mix without pudding
    in the mix
1 cup uncooked old-fashioned oats
²/₃ cup creamy peanut butter
1 egg, slightly beaten
2 tablespoons milk
1 package (8 ounces) cream cheese, softened
1 jar (about 12 ounces) caramel ice cream topping
1 cup semisweet chocolate chips

1. Preheat oven to 350°F. Lightly grease 13×9-inch baking pan.

2. Combine cake mix and oats in large bowl. Cut in peanut butter with pastry blender or 2 knives until mixture is crumbly.

3. Blend egg and milk in small bowl. Add to peanut butter mixture; stir just until combined. Reserve 1½ cups mixture. Press remaining peanut butter mixture into prepared pan.

4. Beat cream cheese in medium bowl with electric mixer at medium speed until fluffy. Add caramel topping; beat just until combined. Carefully spread over peanut butter layer in pan. Crumble reserved peanut butter mixture into small pieces; sprinkle over cream cheese layer. Sprinkle with chocolate chips.

5. Bake 30 minutes or until nearly set in center. Cool completely in pan on wire rack.

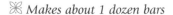

❋ Makes about 1 dozen bars

Cobbled Fruit Bars

1½ **cups apple juice**
1 **cup (6 ounces) chopped dried apricots**
1 **cup (6 ounces) raisins**
1 **package (6 ounces) dried cherries**
1 **teaspoon cornstarch**
1 **teaspoon ground cinnamon**
1 **package (about 18 ounces) yellow cake mix**
2 **cups uncooked old-fashioned oats**
¾ **cup (1½ sticks) butter, melted**
1 **egg**

1. Combine apple juice, apricots, raisins, cherries, cornstarch and cinnamon in medium saucepan, stirring until cornstarch is dissolved. Bring to a boil over medium heat. Boil 5 minutes, stirring constantly. Remove from heat; cool to room temperature.

2. Preheat oven to 350°F. Line 15×10-inch jelly-roll pan with foil and spray lightly with cooking spray.

3. Combine cake mix and oats in large bowl; stir in butter. (Mixture may be dry and clumpy.) Add egg; stir until well blended.

4. Press three-fourths dough mixture into prepared pan. Spread fruit mixture evenly over top. Sprinkle remaining dough mixture over fruit. Bake 25 to 30 minutes or until edges and top are lightly browned. Cool completely in pan on wire rack.

Prep Time: 30 minutes ❋ **Bake Time:** 30 minutes

Candy Bar Bars

¾ cup (1½ sticks) butter or margarine, softened
¼ cup peanut butter
1 cup firmly packed light brown sugar
1 teaspoon baking soda
2 cups uncooked quick-cooking oats
1½ cups all-purpose flour
1 egg
1 (14-ounce) can EAGLE BRAND® Sweetened Condensed Milk
    (NOT evaporated milk)
4 cups chopped candy bars (such as chocolate-covered caramel-topped
    nougat bars with peanuts, chocolate-covered crisp wafers, chocolate-
    covered caramel-topped cookie bars or chocolate-covered peanut
    butter cups)

1. Preheat oven to 350°F. In large bowl, combine butter and peanut butter until smooth; add brown sugar and baking soda. Beat well; stir in oats and flour. Reserve 1¾ cups crumb mixture.

2. Stir egg into remaining crumb mixture in bowl. Press crumb mixture firmly on bottom of ungreased 15×10-inch baking pan. Bake 15 minutes. Remove from oven.

3. Spread EAGLE BRAND® over hot crust. Stir together reserved crumb mixture and candy bar pieces; sprinkle evenly over top.

4. Bake 25 minutes or until golden brown. Cool. Cut into bars. Store leftovers loosely covered at room temperature.

Prep Time: 15 minutes ❋ **Bake Time:** 40 minutes

Hikers' Bar Cookies

³/₄ cup all-purpose flour
¹/₂ cup packed brown sugar
¹/₂ cup uncooked quick oats
¹/₄ cup toasted wheat germ
¹/₄ cup unsweetened applesauce
¹/₄ cup (¹/₂ stick) butter, softened
¹/₈ teaspoon salt
 2 eggs
¹/₄ cup raisins
¹/₄ cup dried cranberries
¹/₄ cup sunflower kernels
 1 tablespoon grated orange peel
 1 teaspoon ground cinnamon

1. Preheat oven to 350°F. Lightly coat 13×9-inch baking pan with nonstick cooking spray; set aside.

2. Beat flour, sugar, oats, wheat germ, applesauce, butter and salt in large bowl with electric mixer at medium speed until well blended. Stir in eggs, raisins, cranberries, sunflower kernels, orange peel and cinnamon. Spread into pan.

3. Bake 15 minutes or until firm. Cool completely in pan on wire rack. Cut into 24 squares.

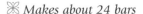

※ Makes about 24 bars

Whole Grain Cereal Bars

    5 to 6 cups assorted whole grain cereals
    1 package (10 ounces) large marshmallows
    ¼ cup (½ stick) butter
    ¼ cup uncooked old-fashioned oats

1. Crush large chunks of cereal by placing in resealable food storage bag and lightly rolling over bag with rolling pin. Grease 13×9-inch baking pan.
2. Heat marshmallows and butter in large saucepan over medium-low heat, stirring until melted and smooth. Remove pan from heat.
3. Stir in cereal until well blended. Using buttered hands or waxed paper to prevent sticking, pat cereal mixture evenly into prepared pan. Sprinkle with oats. Cool at room temperature until firm. Cut into bars.

※ Makes enough dough for 36 bar cookies

Basic Short Dough

    ¾ cup sugar
    ¾ cup (1½ sticks) butter
    1 tablespoon grated lemon peel
    3 egg yolks
    1 teaspoon vanilla
    2 cups all-purpose flour
    ¼ teaspoon salt

Beat sugar, butter and lemon peel in large bowl with electric mixer at medium speed 1 minute. Beat in egg yolks and vanilla until well blended. Scrape down bowl. Add flour and salt; mix just until combined.

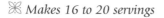

Festive Cranberry Cream Cheese Squares

2 cups all-purpose flour
1½ cups uncooked old-fashioned oats
¾ cup plus 1 tablespoon firmly packed brown sugar, divided
1 cup (2 sticks) butter or margarine, softened
1 (8-ounce) package cream cheese, softened
1 (14-ounce) can EAGLE BRAND® Sweetened Condensed Milk
   (NOT evaporated milk)
2 eggs
1 (27-ounce) jar NONE SUCH® Ready-to-Use Mincemeat
   (Regular or Brandy & Rum)
2 tablespoons cornstarch
1 (16-ounce) can whole-berry cranberry sauce

1. Preheat oven to 375°F. Grease 15×10-inch jellyroll pan. In large bowl, beat flour, oats, ¾ cup brown sugar and butter until crumbly. Reserving 1½ cups crumb mixture, press remaining mixture on bottom of prepared pan. Bake 15 minutes or until lightly browned.
2. In medium bowl, beat cream cheese until fluffy. Gradually beat in EAGLE BRAND® until smooth; beat in eggs. Spread over baked crust; top with NONE SUCH®.
3. Combine remaining 1 tablespoon brown sugar and cornstarch; stir in cranberry sauce. Spoon over mincemeat. Top with reserved crumb mixture. Bake 40 minutes or until golden. Cool. Chill. Cut into squares. Store leftovers covered in refrigerator.

Prep Time: 20 minutes

❋ *Makes about 16 bars*

Chocolate Oatmeal Caramel Bars

1¼ cups uncooked old-fashioned oats
1 cup all-purpose flour
½ cup plus 2 tablespoons packed brown sugar, divided
2 tablespoons unsweetened Dutch process cocoa powder*
¾ cup (1½ sticks) butter, melted
1 can (14 ounces) sweetened condensed milk
⅓ cup butter
½ cup chopped pecans
2 tablespoons powdered sugar

Natural unsweetened cocoa powder may be substituted. Dutch process cocoa powder has a stronger flavor and will bake a darker color.

1. Preheat oven to 350°F. Combine oats, flour, ½ cup brown sugar and cocoa in medium bowl. Add ¾ cup melted butter; mix until crumbly. Reserve 1 cup oat mixture for topping; press remaining oat mixture evenly into bottom of ungreased 8-inch square baking pan. Bake 15 minutes.

2. Combine sweetened condensed milk, ⅓ cup butter and remaining 2 tablespoons brown sugar in medium saucepan; cook and stir over medium heat about 10 minutes or until thick and pale in color.

3. Cool milk mixture slightly until thickened; spread evenly over baked crust. Let stand 5 minutes or until set. Add chopped pecans to reserved oat mixture; sprinkle over caramel layer, patting down gently.

4. Bake 20 minutes or until golden brown. Cool completely in pan on wire rack. Sprinkle with powdered sugar; cut into bars.

Spiked Cheesecake Bars

¹⁄₂ **cup packed light brown sugar**
¹⁄₃ **cup butter, softened**
³⁄₄ **cup plus 1 teaspoon all-purpose flour, divided**
³⁄₄ **cup uncooked quick-cooking oats**
¹⁄₄ **teaspoon baking soda**
  1 **package (8 ounces) cream cheese, softened**
¹⁄₄ **cup granulated sugar**
¹⁄₄ **cup any flavored liqueur, such as coffee, orange or hazelnut**
  2 **tablespoons milk**
  1 **egg**
¹⁄₄ **cup semisweet chocolate chips**

1. Preheat oven to 350°F. Line bottom and sides of 8-inch square baking pan with foil, leaving 2-inch overhang.

2. Beat brown sugar and butter in medium bowl with electric mixer at medium-high speed until creamy. Combine ³⁄₄ cup flour, oats and baking soda in small bowl; gradually beat into sugar mixture at low speed until blended. (Mixture will be crumbly.) Lightly press onto bottom of prepared pan. Bake 20 to 25 minutes or until golden brown.

3. Meanwhile, beat cream cheese, granulated sugar, liqueur and milk with electric mixer at medium-high speed until smooth. Add egg and remaining 1 teaspoon flour; beat until well blended. Spoon filling over hot crust. Bake 40 minutes or until set. Cool completely in pan on wire rack.

4. Place chocolate chips in small resealable food storage bag; microwave on HIGH 1 minute or until slightly melted. Knead bag; microwave 20 seconds or until completely melted. Cut tiny hole in one corner of bag and drizzle chocolate over cooled cheesecake. Cover with foil and refrigerate overnight for best flavor and texture.

Oats of Wisdom: When cutting cheesecake, wipe the knife blade between cuts for smoother, neater edges.

❋ Makes 24 bars

O'Henrietta Bars

MAZOLA PURE® Cooking Spray
½ cup (1 stick) butter or margarine, softened
½ cup packed brown sugar
½ cup KARO® Light or Dark Corn Syrup
1 teaspoon vanilla
3 cups quick oats, uncooked
½ cup (3 ounces) semi-sweet chocolate chips
¼ cup creamy peanut butter

1. Preheat oven to 350°F. Spray 8- or 9-inch square baking pan with cooking spray.
2. Beat butter, brown sugar, corn syrup and vanilla in large bowl with mixer at medium speed until smooth. Stir in oats. Press into prepared pan.
3. Bake 25 minutes or until center is barely firm. Cool on wire rack 5 minutes.
4. Sprinkle with chocolate chips; top with small spoonfuls of peanut butter. Let stand 5 minutes; spread peanut butter and chocolate over bars, swirling to marble.
5. Cool completely on wire rack before cutting. Cut into bars; refrigerate 15 minutes to set topping.

Prep Time: 20 minutes ❋ **Bake Time:** 25 minutes, plus cooling

Super Snackable Cakes

Cherry-Almond Streusel Cake

CAKE
1½ cups biscuit baking mix
½ cup milk
2 eggs
2 tablespoons granulated sugar
2 tablespoons vegetable oil
1 teaspoon vanilla
¼ teaspoon almond extract
½ to ¾ cup dried cherries

TOPPING
½ cup slivered almonds
½ cup uncooked old-fashioned oats
⅓ cup biscuit baking mix
⅓ cup packed dark brown sugar
¼ teaspoon ground cinnamon
3 tablespoons cold butter, cubed

1. Preheat oven to 375° F. Spray 8-inch round baking pan with nonstick cooking spray.

2. Combine all cake ingredients, except cherries, in medium bowl. Stir until well blended. Gently stir in cherries. Spread batter into prepared pan; set aside.

3. Combine all topping ingredients, except butter, in medium bowl. Cut in butter with pastry blender or two knives until butter is the size of peas.

4. Sprinkle topping evenly over batter. Bake 18 to 20 minutes or until toothpick inserted into center comes out almost clean. Let stand at least 30 minutes before serving.

Oats of Wisdom: Any dried fruit, such as cranberries or raisins, may be substituted.

✳ ✳ ✳

＊ ＊ ＊

Caramel-Topped Cheesecakes with Oat-Pecan Crust

1½ cups QUAKER® Oats (quick or old fashioned), uncooked
½ cup finely chopped pecans
1¼ cups packed light brown sugar, divided
¼ cup butter or margarine, melted
2 packages (8 ounces each) cream cheese, softened
1 teaspoon vanilla
3 eggs, at room temperature
½ cup sour cream
¾ cup butterscotch caramel topping
Sea salt

1. Heat oven to 375°F. Line 18 medium muffin cups with foil liners.

2. Combine oats, pecans, ½ cup brown sugar and butter in large bowl, blending well. Spoon about 2 tablespoons of mixture into bottom of each foil-lined muffin cup, then press evenly and firmly to form crust. Bake 8 to 10 minutes or until golden brown. Remove from oven and cool.

3. Reduce oven temperature to 325°F. Beat cream cheese in large bowl with electric mixer at medium-high speed until light and fluffy, scraping bowl occasionally. Add remaining ¾ cup brown sugar and vanilla; blend well. Add eggs, one at a time, beating just until blended. Add sour cream; mix well. Divide batter evenly among prepared muffin cups. Bake about 20 to 22 minutes, or just until set. Cool in pans on wire rack. Chill at least 2 hours.

4. Just before serving, top each individual cheesecake with scant tablespoon of butterscotch caramel topping (if too thick to spread, place in microwave for a few seconds to soften). Sprinkle with sea salt and serve.

* * *

Sweet Potato Crumb Cakes

¹/₂ **cup granulated sugar**
   Grated peel of 1 orange
¹/₂ **cup chopped pecans**
  1 **teaspoon ground cinnamon**
¹/₄ **cup all-purpose flour**
¹/₄ **cup oats**
¹/₄ **cup (¹/₂ stick) cold butter, cut into 4 pieces**
  1 **package (16 ounces) Sweet Potato Pound Cake mix, plus ingredients to prepare mix**
   Powdered sugar (optional)

1. Preheat oven to 350°F. Spray six individual loaf pans or 8 standard (2¹/₂-inch) muffin cups with nonstick cooking spray.

2. Combine granulated sugar and orange peel in food processor. Pulse several times to thoroughly mix. Add pecans and cinnamon; pulse until pecans are the size of peas. Reserve ¹/₃ cup of crumb mixture and set aside. Add flour, oats and butter to remaining crumb mixture; pulse until butter is the size of peas; set aside.

3. Prepare cake mix according to package directions. Divide batter in half. Pour half of batter evenly into prepared pans. Sprinkle with ¹/₃ cup reserved crumb mixture. Carefully spoon remaining batter evenly over crumb mixture. Top with remaining crumb mixture.

4. Bake 25 to 30 minutes or until toothpick inserted into centers comes out clean. Cool in pans 15 minutes. Remove to wire rack; cool completely. Dust with powdered sugar, if desired.

✳ *Makes one (9-inch) cheesecake*

Apple Cinnamon Cheesecake

1/2 cup (1 stick) plus 1 tablespoon butter or margarine, softened and
  divided
1/4 cup firmly packed light brown sugar
 1 cup all-purpose flour
1/4 cup quick-cooking oats
1/4 cup finely chopped walnuts
1/2 teaspoon ground cinnamon
 2 (8-ounce) packages cream cheese, softened
 1 (14-ounce) can EAGLE BRAND® Sweetened Condensed Milk
   (NOT evaporated milk)
 3 eggs
1/2 cup frozen apple juice concentrate, thawed
 2 medium apples, cored and sliced
   Cinnamon Apple Glaze (recipe follows)

1. Preheat over to 300°F. In small bowl, beat 1/2 cup butter and brown sugar
until fluffy. Add flour, oats, walnuts and cinnamon; mix well. Press firmly on
bottom and halfway up side of 9-inch springform pan. Bake 10 minutes.
2. In large bowl, beat cream cheese until fluffy. Gradually beat in EAGLE
BRAND® until smooth. Add eggs and apple juice concentrate; mix well. Pour
into baked crust.
3. Bake 45 minutes or until center springs back when lightly touched. Cool.
4. In large skillet, cook apples in remaining 1 tablespoon butter until tender-
crisp. Arrange on top of cheesecake; drizzle with Cinnamon Apple Glaze. Chill.
Store leftovers covered in refrigerator.

Prep Time: 20 minutes

✳ *Makes about 1/4 cup*

Cinnamon Apple Glaze

1/4 cup frozen apple juice concentrate, thawed
 1 teaspoon cornstarch
1/4 teaspoon ground cinnamon

In small saucepan, combine ingredients; mix well. Over low heat, cook and stir
until thickened.

Tropical Snack Cake

1½ cups all-purpose flour
1 cup QUAKER® Oats (quick or old fashioned, uncooked)
¼ cup granulated sugar or 2 tablespoons fructose
2 teaspoons baking powder
½ teaspoon baking soda
¼ teaspoon salt (optional)
1 can (8 ounces) crushed pineapple in juice, undrained
½ cup fat-free milk
⅓ cup mashed ripe banana
¼ cup egg substitute or 2 egg whites
2 tablespoons vegetable oil
2 teaspoons vanilla

Heat oven to 350°F. Grease and flour 8×8-inch square baking pan. Combine first 6 ingredients; mix well. Set aside. Blend pineapple, milk, banana, egg substitute, oil and vanilla until mixed thoroughly. Add to dry ingredients, mixing just until moistened. Pour into prepared pan. Bake 45 to 50 minutes or until golden brown and wooden pick inserted in center comes out clean. Cool slightly before serving.

✳ *Makes about 24 servings*

Oat-Apricot Snack Cake

1 container (8 ounces) plain yogurt
³/₄ cup packed brown sugar
¹/₂ cup granulated sugar
¹/₃ cup vegetable oil
1 egg
4 tablespoons milk, divided
2 teaspoons vanilla
1 cup all-purpose flour
¹/₂ cup whole wheat flour
1 teaspoon baking soda
1 teaspoon ground cinnamon
¹/₂ teaspoon salt
2 cups uncooked old-fashioned oats
1 cup (about 6 ounces) chopped dried apricots
1 cup powdered sugar

1. Preheat oven to 350°F. Spray 13×9-inch baking pan with nonstick cooking spray. Stir yogurt, sugars, oil, egg, 2 tablespoons milk and vanilla in large bowl until thoroughly mixed.

2. Sift flours, baking soda, cinnamon and salt in medium bowl. Add dry ingredients to wet ingredients; mix well. Stir in oats and apricots until well mixed.

3. Spread batter in prepared pan. Bake 25 to 30 minutes or until toothpick inserted into center comes out clean. Cool completely in pan on wire rack.

4. Stir powdered sugar and remaining 2 tablespoons milk in small bowl until smooth. Spoon glaze into small resealable food storage bag. Seal bag and cut ¹/₄ inch from one corner; drizzle glaze over bars.

Chocolate-Peanut Butter Oatmeal Snacking Cake

1¼ **cups boiling water**
  1 **cup uncooked old-fashioned oats**
  1 **cup granulated sugar**
  1 **cup packed brown sugar**
 ½ **cup (1 stick) butter, softened**
  2 **eggs, beaten**
  1 **teaspoon vanilla**
1¾ **cups all-purpose flour**
 ¼ **cup unsweetened cocoa powder**
  1 **teaspoon baking soda**
  1 **cup semisweet chocolate chips**
  1 **package (12 ounces) chocolate and peanut butter chips**

1. Preheat oven to 350°F. Grease 13×9-inch baking pan.
2. Combine boiling water and oats in medium bowl; let stand 10 minutes. Stir until water is absorbed. Add sugars and butter; beat with electric mixer at low speed 1 minute or until well blended. Add eggs and vanilla; beat well.
3. Combine flour, cocoa and baking soda in medium bowl. Gradually beat into oat mixture until well blended. Stir in 1 cup chocolate chips. Pour into prepared pan. Sprinkle chocolate and peanut butter chips over top.
4. Bake 40 minutes or until toothpick inserted into center comes out clean. Cool completely in pan on wire rack.

✳ *Makes about 9 servings*

Topsy-Turvy Banana Crunch Cake

⅓ **cup uncooked old-fashioned oats**
3 **tablespoons packed brown sugar**
1 **tablespoon all-purpose flour**
¼ **teaspoon ground cinnamon**
2 **tablespoons butter**
2 **tablespoons chopped pecans**
1 **package (9 ounces) yellow cake mix without pudding in the mix**
½ **cup sour cream**
½ **cup mashed banana (about 1 medium)**
1 **egg, slightly beaten**
½ **cup pecan halves (optional)**

1. Preheat oven to 350°F. Lightly grease 8-inch square baking pan.
2. Combine oats, brown sugar, flour and cinnamon in small bowl. Cut in butter with pastry blender or two knives until crumbly. Stir in chopped pecans.
3. Beat cake mix, sour cream, banana and egg in medium bowl with electric mixer at low speed about 1 minute or until blended. Beat at medium speed 1 to 2 minutes or until smooth. Spoon half of batter into prepared pan; sprinkle with half of oat mixture. Top with remaining batter and oat mixture. Sprinkle with pecan halves, if desired.
4. Bake 25 to 30 minutes or until toothpick inserted into center comes out clean. Cool completely in pan on wire rack.

Main Dish Magic

※ *Makes 4 to 6 servings*

Turkey Meat Loaf

1 pound ground turkey
¾ cup uncooked quick oats
1 cup tomato sauce, divided
1 small onion, finely chopped
1 egg
1 teaspoon salt

1. Preheat oven to 350°F. Spray 9×5-inch loaf pan with nonstick cooking spray.

2. Combine turkey, oats, ½ cup tomato sauce, onion, egg and salt in large bowl; mix well. Shape into loaf; place in prepared pan.

3. Bake 45 minutes to 1 hour or until browned and cooked through (165°F). Top with remaining sauce; bake 5 minutes. Remove from pan; cut into slices.

Note: Ketchup or salsa can be substituted for the tomato sauce.

> Oats of Wisdom: After removing the baked meat loaf from the oven, run knife around the edges, then let it stand for 10 minutes. This allows the meat loaf to set and will make slicing easier.

Chicken and Veggie Meatballs with Fennel

1 pound ground chicken
$^1/_2$ cup finely chopped green onion
$^1/_2$ cup finely chopped green bell pepper
$^1/_3$ cup oatmeal
$^1/_4$ cup grated Parmesan cheese
$^1/_4$ cup shredded carrots
2 egg whites
2 garlic cloves, minced
$^1/_2$ teaspoon dried Italian seasoning
$^1/_4$ teaspoon salt
$^1/_4$ teaspoon dried fennel seed
$^1/_8$ teaspoon red pepper flakes (optional)
1 teaspoon extra-virgin olive oil
Pasta sauce

1. Combine all ingredients except oil and pasta sauce in large mixing bowl. Shape into 36 balls, each about 1 inch in diameter.

2. Heat oil in large nonstick skillet over medium-high heat. Add meatballs; cook 10 minutes or until no longer pink in center, turning frequently. Use fork and spoon for easy turning. Serve immediately with pasta sauce.

Note: To freeze meatballs, cool completely and place in large freezer resealable food storage bag. Release any excess air from bag and seal. Freeze bag flat for easier storage and faster thawing. To thaw, remove amount of meatballs needed from freezer bag and reseal bag, releasing any excess air. Place meatballs on a microwavable plate and cook on HIGH 20 to 30 seconds.

Mu Shu Meatball Wraps

MEATBALLS

1 pound lean ground turkey or lean ground beef
3/4 cup QUAKER® Oats (quick or old fashioned, uncooked)
1/2 cup finely chopped water chestnuts
1/3 cup chopped green onions
1 clove garlic, minced
1 teaspoon finely chopped fresh ginger *or* 1/4 teaspoon ground ginger
1/4 cup light soy sauce
1 tablespoon water

WRAPS

3/4 cup prepared plum sauce
6 (10-inch) flour tortillas, warmed
1 1/2 cups coleslaw mix or combination of shredded cabbage and
    shredded carrots

1. Heat oven to 350°F. Combine all meatball ingredients in large bowl; mix lightly but thoroughly. Shape into 24 (1 1/2-inch) meatballs; arrange on rack of broiler pan.

2. Bake 20 to 25 minutes or until centers are no longer pink (170°F for turkey; 160°F for beef).

3. To prepare wraps, spread plum sauce on flour tortilla; add about 1/4 cup coleslaw mix and 4 hot meatballs. Fold sides of tortilla to center, overlapping edges; fold bottom and top of tortilla under, completely enclosing filling. Repeat with remaining ingredients. Cut wrap in half to serve.

※ Makes 4 servings

Spicy Oat-Crusted Chicken with Sunshine Salsa

SUNSHINE SALSA
- ³/₄ **cup prepared salsa**
- ³/₄ **cup coarsely chopped orange sections**

CHICKEN
- 2 **tablespoons canola oil**
- 1 **tablespoon margarine, melted**
- 2 **teaspoons chili powder**
- 1 **teaspoon garlic powder**
- 1 **teaspoon ground cumin**
- ³/₄ **teaspoon salt**
- 1¹/₂ **cups Quick QUAKER® Oats, uncooked**
- 1 **egg, lightly beaten**
- 1 **tablespoon water**
- 4 **boneless, skinless chicken breast halves (about 5 to 6 ounces each)**
  Chopped fresh cilantro (optional)

1. Combine salsa and orange sections in small bowl. Refrigerate, covered, until serving time.

2. Heat oven to 375°F. Line baking sheet with aluminum foil. Stir together oil, margarine, chili powder, garlic powder, cumin and salt in flat, shallow dish. Add oats, stirring until evenly moistened.

3. Beat egg and water with fork until frothy in second flat, shallow dish. Dip chicken into egg mixture, then coat completely in seasoned oats. Place chicken on foil-lined baking sheet. Pat any extra oat mixture onto top of chicken.

4. Bake 30 minutes or until chicken is cooked through and oat coating is golden brown. Serve with salsa. Garnish with cilantro, if desired.

Old-Fashioned Meat Loaf

1 teaspoon olive oil
1 cup finely chopped onion
4 cloves garlic, minced
1½ pounds ground beef
1 cup chili sauce, divided
¾ cup uncooked old-fashioned oats
2 egg whites
½ teaspoon black pepper
¼ teaspoon salt
1 tablespoon Dijon mustard

1. Preheat oven to 375°F. Heat oil in large nonstick skillet over medium heat. Add onion; cook and stir 5 minutes. Add garlic; cook 1 minute. Remove from heat; transfer to large bowl. Let cool 5 minutes.

2. Add beef, ½ cup chili sauce, oats, egg whites, pepper and salt; mix well. Pack into 9×5-inch loaf pan. Combine remaining ½ cup chili sauce and mustard in small bowl; spoon evenly over top of meat loaf.

3. Bake 45 to 50 minutes or until cooked through (160°F). Let stand 5 minutes. Pour off any juices from pan. Cut into slices to serve.

Nancy's Grilled Turkey Meatballs

1 pound lean ground turkey breast
1/2 cup uncooked old-fashioned oats
1/4 cup fresh whole wheat bread crumbs
1 egg white
3 tablespoons Parmesan cheese
2 tablespoons *French's*® Honey Dijon Mustard
1/4 teaspoon crushed garlic
1/4 teaspoon ground black pepper
1 cup pineapple chunks or wedges
1 small red bell pepper, cut into squares

1. Combine turkey, oats, bread crumbs, egg white, cheese, mustard, garlic and black pepper in large bowl. Mix well and form into 24 meatballs.

2. Place 4 meatballs on each skewer, alternating with pineapple and bell pepper.

3. Cook meatballs 10 minutes on well-greased grill over medium heat until no longer pink inside, turning often. Serve with additional *French's*® Honey Dijon Mustard on the side for dipping.

Prep Time: 15 minutes ※ **Cook Time:** 10 minutes

> Oats of Wisdom: Combine 1/3 cup each *French's*®
> Honey Dijon Mustard, honey and *Frank's*® *RedHot*®
> Cayenne Pepper Sauce. Use for dipping grilled wings, ribs
> and chicken.

Acknowledgments

The publisher would like to thank the companies listed below
for the use of their recipes in this publication.

ACH Food Companies, Inc.

Dole Food Company, Inc.

EAGLE BRAND®

The Hershey Company

©Mars, Incorporated 2009

Minnesota Cultivated Wild Rice Council

Nestlé USA

The Quaker® Oatmeal Kitchens

Reckitt Benckiser Inc.

Riviana Foods Inc.

The Sugar Association, Inc.

A

Almonds
Baked Cherry-Almond Oatmeal, 62
Cherry-Almond Streusel Cake, 116
Chunky-Fruity Homemade Granola, 66
Cranberry Peach Almond Dessert, 76
Fruited Granola, 52
Honey Granola with Yogurt, 56

Apple
Apple Cinnamon Cheesecake, 122
Apple Cinnamon Rice Crisp, 72
Apple Crumble Pot, 74
Apple-Date Upside-Down Tart, 81
Apple Toffee Crisp, 86
Baked Oatmeal with Apricots, 55
Carrot and Oat Muffins, 18
Cinnamon Apple Glaze, 122
Cinnamon Pear Crisp, 82
Cobbled Fruit Bars, 102
Harvest Apple Oatmeal, 63
Hikers' Bar Cookies, 105
Oats 'n' Apple Tart, 78
Sunny Seed Bran Waffles, 50

Apricots
Baked Oatmeal with Apricots, 55
Chunky-Fruity Homemade Granola, 66
Cobbled Fruit Bars, 102
Oat-Apricot Snack Cake, 124

B

Baked Cherry-Almond Oatmeal, 62
Baked Oatmeal with Apricots, 55

Banana
Banana Bread Oatmeal, 54
Banana-Nana Pecan Bread, 15
Fruited Granola, 52
Good Morning Bread, 20
Hearty Banana Carrot Muffins, 6
Topsy-Turvy Banana Crunch Cake, 128
Tropical Fruit Breakfast Parfaits, 48

Basic Oatmeal Cookies, 41
Basic Short Dough, 106
Beef: Old-Fashioned Meat Loaf, 136

Blueberries
Chunky-Fruity Homemade Granola, 66
Fruited Granola, 52
Peach and Blueberry Crisp, 84

Butterscotch
Butterscotch Oatmeal Cookies, 30

Caramel-Topped Cheesecakes with Oat-Pecan Crust, 118
Fudgy Oatmeal Butterscotch Cookies, 38

C

Cake Mix
Cobbled Fruit Bars, 102
Fudgy Oatmeal Butterscotch Cookies, 38
Ooey-Gooey Caramel Peanut Butter Bars, 100
Sweet Potato Crumb Cakes, 120
Topsy-Turvy Banana Crunch Cake, 128

Candy
Candy Bar Bars, 104
Fudgy Oatmeal Butterscotch Cookies, 38
Spiky Hedgehogs, 32
Caramel-Nut Sticky Biscuits, 64
Caramel-Topped Cheesecakes with Oat-Pecan Crust, 118

Carrots
Carrot and Oat Muffins, 18
Hearty Banana Carrot Muffins, 6
Savory Summertime Oat Bread, 14

Cherry
Baked Cherry-Almond Oatmeal, 62
Cherry-Almond Streusel Cake, 116
Chunky-Fruity Homemade Granola, 66
Cobbled Fruit Bars, 102
Double Cherry Crumbles, 90
Oat and Whole Wheat Scones, 10

Chicken
Chicken and Veggie Meatballs with Fennel, 132
Spicy Oat-Crusted Chicken with Sunshine Salsa, 135

Chocolate
Chocolate 'n' Oat Bars, 98
Chocolate Oatmeal Caramel Bars, 110
Chocolate Oatmeal Chippers, 26
Chocolate-Peanut Butter Oatmeal Snacking Cake, 126
Cookie Dough Bears, 38
Double Chocolate Coconut Oatmeal Cookies, 42
Double Striped Peanut Butter Oatmeal Cookies, 44

Chocolate *(continued)*
Oat, Chocolate and Hazelnut Biscotti, 34
Oatmeal-Chip Crispies, 36
Oatmeal S'Mores Cookies, 47
O'Henrietta Bars, 114
Ooey-Gooey Caramel Peanut Butter Bars, 100
Spiky Hedgehogs, 32
Chunky-Fruity Homemade Granola, 66
Cinnamon Apple Glaze, 122
Cinnamon Pear Crisp, 82
Cobbled Fruit Bars, 102
Coconut
Butterscotch Oatmeal Cookies, 30
Chunky-Fruity Homemade Granola, 66
Cranberry Coconut Bars, 94
Double Chocolate Coconut Oatmeal Cookies, 42
Spiky Hedgehogs, 32
Tropical Fruit Breakfast Parfaits, 48
Cookie Dough Bears, 38
Cranberries
Apple Crumble Pot, 74
Chunky-Fruity Homemade Granola, 66
Cranberry Coconut Bars, 94
Cranberry Peach Almond Dessert, 76
Festive Cranberry Cream Cheese Squares, 108
Fruited Granola, 52
Oatmeal-Chip Crispies, 36
Cranberry Coconut Bars, 94
Cranberry Peach Almond Dessert, 76

D
Dates
Apple-Date Upside-Down Tart, 81
Good Morning Bread, 20
Oatmeal Date Bars, 92
Double Cherry Crumbles, 90
Double Chocolate Coconut Oatmeal Cookies, 42
Double Striped Peanut Butter Oatmeal Cookies, 44

F
Festive Cranberry Cream Cheese Squares, 108
Fruited Granola, 52
Fudgy Oatmeal Butterscotch Cookies, 38

G
Gingery Oat and Molasses Cookies, 28
Good Morning Bread, 20
Grandma's Old-Fashioned Oatmeal Cookies, 46

H
Harvest Apple Oatmeal, 63
Hearty Banana Carrot Muffins, 6
Hikers' Bar Cookies, 105
Honey Granola with Yogurt, 56

M
Marshmallows
Oatmeal S'Mores Cookies, 47
Whole Grain Cereal Bars, 106
Mixed Berry Crunch7, 80
Muffins
Carrot and Oat Muffins, 18
Hearty Banana Carrot Muffins, 6
Strawberry Muffins, 12
Mu Shu Meatball Wraps, 134

N
Nancy's Grilled Turkey Meatballs, 138
No-Knead Sandwich Bread, 8

O
Oat and Whole Wheat Scones, 10
Oat-Apricot Snack Cake, 124
Oatmeal Brûlée with Raspberry Sauce, 68
Oatmeal-Chip Crispies, 36
Oat, Chocolate and Hazelnut Biscotti, 34
Oatmeal Crème Brûlée, 60
Oatmeal Date Bars, 92
Oatmeal Pecan Pancakes, 58
Oatmeal S'Mores Cookies, 47
Oats 'n' Apple Tart, 78
O'Henrietta Bars, 114
Old-Fashioned Meat Loaf, 136
Ooey-Gooey Caramel Peanut Butter Bars, 100

P
PB & J Thumbprint Cookies, 40
Peach
Cranberry Peach Almond Dessert, 76
Peach and Blueberry Crisp, 84
Strawberry and Peach Crisp, 70

Peanut Butter
   Chocolate-Peanut Butter Oatmeal
      Snacking Cake, 126
   Double Striped Peanut Butter
      Oatmeal Cookies, 44
   Ooey-Gooey Caramel Peanut Butter
      Bars, 100
   PB & J Thumbprint Cookies, 40
   Spiky Hedgehogs, 32
Pear
   Cinnamon Pear Crisp, 82
   Pear Hazelnut Bars, 96
Pecans
   Apple Crumble Pot, 74
   Banana-Nana Pecan Bread, 15
   Butterscotch Oatmeal Cookies, 30
   Caramel-Nut Sticky Biscuits, 64
   Caramel-Topped Cheesecakes with
      Oat-Pecan Crust, 118
   Chocolate Oatmeal Caramel Bars,
      110
   Cranberry Coconut Bars, 94
   Double Cherry Crumbles, 90
   Oatmeal Pecan Pancakes, 58
   Sweet Potato Crumb Cakes, 120
Pineapple
   Nancy's Grilled Turkey Meatballs,
      138
   Pineapple Oatmeal Cookies, 31
   Tropical Fruit Breakfast Parfaits, 48
   Tropical Snack Cake, 123
Pumpkin Oatmeal Cookies, 24

R
Raisins
   Apple Cinnamon Rice Crisp, 72
   Cinnamon Pear Crisp, 82
   Cobbled Fruit Bars, 102
   Grandma's Old-Fashioned Oatmeal
      Cookies, 46
   Pear Hazelnut Bars, 96
   Pineapple Oatmeal Cookies, 31
Raspberries: Oatmeal Brûlée with
      Raspberry Sauce, 68
Refrigerated Cookie Dough
   Cookie Dough Bears, 38
   Double Cherry Crumbles, 90
   Oatmeal Date Bars, 92
   Spiky Hedgehogs, 32
Rhubarb Tart, 82

Rice
   Apple Cinnamon Rice Crisp, 72
   Wild Rice Three Grain Bread, 16
Rustic Plum Tart, 88

S
Savory Summertime Oat Bread, 14
Soda Bread, 22
Spicy Oat-Crusted Chicken with
      Sunshine Salsa, 135
Spiked Cheesecake Bars, 112
Spiky Hedgehogs, 32
Strawberry
   Honey Granola with Yogurt, 56
   Strawberry and Peach Crisp, 70
   Strawberry Muffins, 12
   Tropical Fruit Breakfast Parfaits, 48
Sunny Seed Bran Waffles, 50
Sweet Potato Crumb Cakes, 120

T
Three-Grain Bread, 4
Topsy-Turvy Banana Crunch Cake, 128
Tropical Fruit Breakfast Parfaits, 48
Tropical Snack Cake, 123
Turkey
   Mu Shu Meatball Wraps, 134
   Nancy's Grilled Turkey Meatballs, 138
   Turkey Meat Loaf, 130
W
Walnuts
   Apple Cinnamon Rice Crisp, 72
   Gingery Oat and Molasses Cookies,
      28
Whole Grain Cereal Bars, 106
Wild Rice Three Grain Bread, 16

Y
Yeast Breads
   Good Morning Bread, 20
   No-Knead Sandwich Bread, 8
   Savory Summertime Oat Bread, 14
   Three-Grain Bread, 4
   Wild Rice Three Grain Bread, 16
Yogurt
   Honey Granola with Yogurt, 56
   Oat-Apricot Snack Cake, 124
   Tropical Fruit Breakfast Parfaits, 48

METRIC CONVERSION CHART

VOLUME MEASUREMENTS (dry)

$\frac{1}{8}$ teaspoon = 0.5 mL
$\frac{1}{4}$ teaspoon = 1 mL
$\frac{1}{2}$ teaspoon = 2 mL
$\frac{3}{4}$ teaspoon = 4 mL
1 teaspoon = 5 mL
1 tablespoon = 15 mL
2 tablespoons = 30 mL
$\frac{1}{4}$ cup = 60 mL
$\frac{1}{3}$ cup = 75 mL
$\frac{1}{2}$ cup = 125 mL
$\frac{2}{3}$ cup = 150 mL
$\frac{3}{4}$ cup = 175 mL
1 cup = 250 mL
2 cups = 1 pint = 500 mL
3 cups = 750 mL
4 cups = 1 quart = 1 L

VOLUME MEASUREMENTS (fluid)

1 fluid ounce (2 tablespoons) = 30 mL
4 fluid ounces ($\frac{1}{2}$ cup) = 125 mL
8 fluid ounces (1 cup) = 250 mL
12 fluid ounces ($1\frac{1}{2}$ cups) = 375 mL
16 fluid ounces (2 cups) = 500 mL

WEIGHTS (mass)

$\frac{1}{2}$ ounce = 15 g
1 ounce = 30 g
3 ounces = 90 g
4 ounces = 120 g
8 ounces = 225 g
10 ounces = 285 g
12 ounces = 360 g
16 ounces = 1 pound = 450 g

DIMENSIONS

$\frac{1}{16}$ inch = 2 mm
$\frac{1}{8}$ inch = 3 mm
$\frac{1}{4}$ inch = 6 mm
$\frac{1}{2}$ inch = 1.5 cm
$\frac{3}{4}$ inch = 2 cm
1 inch = 2.5 cm

OVEN TEMPERATURES

250°F = 120°C
275°F = 140°C
300°F = 150°C
325°F = 160°C
350°F = 180°C
375°F = 190°C
400°F = 200°C
425°F = 220°C
450°F = 230°C

BAKING PAN SIZES

Utensil	Size in Inches/Quarts	Metric Volume	Size in Centimeters
Baking or	$8 \times 8 \times 2$	2 L	$20 \times 20 \times 5$
Cake Pan	$9 \times 9 \times 2$	2.5 L	$23 \times 23 \times 5$
(square or	$12 \times 8 \times 2$	3 L	$30 \times 20 \times 5$
rectangular)	$13 \times 9 \times 2$	3.5 L	$33 \times 23 \times 5$
Loaf Pan	$8 \times 4 \times 3$	1.5 L	$20 \times 10 \times 7$
	$9 \times 5 \times 3$	2 L	$23 \times 13 \times 7$
Round Layer	$8 \times 1\frac{1}{2}$	1.2 L	20×4
Cake Pan	$9 \times 1\frac{1}{2}$	1.5 L	23×4
Pie Plate	$8 \times 1\frac{1}{4}$	750 mL	20×3
	$9 \times 1\frac{1}{4}$	1 L	23×3
Baking Dish	1 quart	1 L	—
or Casserole	$1\frac{1}{2}$ quart	1.5 L	—
	2 quart	2 L	—